RON,

THANKS FOR YOUR

LEADERSHIP IN PURSUING OUR

AVIATION GOALS.

Bill

9/16/94

Best Laid Plans

William B. Rouse
Search Technology

P T R Prentice Hall
Englewood Cliffs, New Jersey 07632

Library of Congress Cataloging-in-Publication Data

```
Rouse, William B.
     Best laid plans / William B. Rouse.
        p.  cm,
     Includes index.
     ISBN 0-13-300054-0
     1. Planning 2. Corporate planning 3. New products--Planning.
  I.Title
  HD30.28.R674  1995                        94-16433
  658.4'012--dc20                              CIP
```

Editorial/production supervision
  and interior design: *Ann Sullivan*
Chapter opening design: *Gail Cocker-Bogusz*
Cover design: *Tommyboy Graphics*
Cover photo: *J. A. Kraulis/Master File*
Manufacturing manager: *Alexis R. Heydt*
Acquisitions editor: *Bernard Goodwin*
Editorial assistant: *Diane Spina*

©1994 by P T R Prentice Hall
Prentice-Hall, Inc.
A Paramount Communications Company
Englewood Cliffs, New Jersey 07632

The publisher offers discounts on this book when ordered in bulk quantities. For more information, contact:

Corporate Sales Department
PTR Prentice Hall
113 Sylvan Avenue
Englewood Cliffs, NJ 07632

Phone: 201-592-2863
Fax: 201-592-2249

Printed in the United States of America

10 9 8 7 6 5 4 3 2 1

ISBN 0-13-300054-0

Prentice-Hall International (UK) Limited, *London*
Prentice-Hall of Australia Pty. Limited, *Sydney*
Prentice-Hall Canada Inc., *Toronto*
Prentice-Hall Hispanoamericana, S.A., *Mexico*
Prentice-Hall of India Private Limited, *New Delhi*
Prentice-Hall of Japan, Inc., *Tokyo*
Simon & Schuster Asia Pte. Ltd., *Singapore*
Editora Prentice-Hall do Brasil, Ltda., *Rio de Janeiro*

BOOKS BY WILLIAM B. ROUSE

Best Laid Plans

Catalysts for Change:
Concepts and Principles for Enabling Change

Strategies for Innovation:
Creating Successful Products, Systems,and Organizations

Design for Success:
A Human-Centered Approach to Creating Successful Products and
Systems

Systems Engineering Models of Human-Machine Interaction

Management of Library Networks:
Policy Analysis, Implementation, and Control
(with S. H. Rouse)

EDITED BOOKS

Human / Technology Interaction in Complex Systems
(Seven Volumes)

Robotics, Control, and Society
(with N. Moray and W. R. Ferrell)

System Design:
Behavioral Perspectives on Designers, Tools, and Organizations
(with K.R. Boff)

Human Detection and Diagnosis of System Failures
(with J. Rasmussen)

Contents

v

Preface

For many years, I have been fascinated with people's abilities and inclinations to plan. In the 1970s and 1980s, this fascination led to studies of aircraft pilots, air traffic controllers, nuclear power plant operators, supertanker crews, library network managers, and design engineers. These studies focused on people's problem solving abilities and limitations, as well as on the role of planning in the process of problem solving.

In the late 1980s and early 1990s, I focused on how enterprises plan new products, systems, and services. These efforts also focused on the enterprises' plans for themselves, including their visions for their relationships with the marketplace, their organizational structures, and the overall nature of their operations. These efforts culminated in three books. *Design for Success*, published in 1991, focuses on product planning. *Strategies for Innovation*, in 1992, is concerned with business planning. The third book, *Catalysts for Change*, 1993, considers the nature of changes in markets and organizations and how such changes can be facilitated.

In seminars, workshops, and consulting efforts for roughly 100 enterprises, involving approximately 2,000 people, I have employed the concepts, principles, methods, and tools described in these books. The integrated methodologies and associated computer tools have been very well received. An increasing number of enterprises are using the approaches embodied in these methods and tools.

While this might seem to be an unqualified "success story," I have encountered several problems. One difficulty is that the structured, multistep methodologies described in these books tend to be overwhelming for many potential users. Many people are not used to being as systematic and comprehensive as these approaches tend to require. Consequently, the use of these approaches often involves much more effort than many people are willing to invest.

Another difficulty is most people's relative lack of familiarity with computer-based planning tools for other than financial planning. Computer-based tools can assume the burden of being systematic and comprehensive. However, this type of support is perceived as useful only by those who feel comfortable relying on computers.

Repeated encounters with these difficulties led me to consider how the essence of the approaches presented in these three books could be explained in a much less technical manner. The range of applications for the concepts and principles in these books has included intelligent software systems for aircraft, design tools for engineers, large-scale passenger reservation systems, point-of-sale terminals for clothing stores, new high-nutrition tomatoes, and hot water heaters for developing countries. As I reflected on these and other applications, I wondered how the "nuggets" of wisdom embodied in these approaches could be illustrated in contexts much simpler than airplanes, power and process plants, and design offices. These musings led to this book.

My goal in this book is to illustrate the universality of planning difficulties and the simplicity of basic concepts and principles that can enhance the efficiency and effectiveness of planning. This goal is pursued through discussion and exploration of three types of planning problem—product planning, business planning, and life planning. Put simply, these three types of planning deal, respectively, with the questions of what to sell, how to organize, and what to become.

These questions are pursued by considering three metaphors: woodworking, hiking, and discovery. Woodworking—designing and manufacturing furniture—is used as a metaphor for all product planning. Hiking—planning and making mountain treks—is employed as a metaphor for all business planning. Discovery—uncovering and understanding other cultures and societies—is used as a metaphor for all life planning. By employing these metaphors, it is possible to explain and illustrate concepts and principles of planning in simple, concrete ways. These metaphors also provide the means for exploring the philosophical underpinnings of planning.

Earlier I referred to nuggets of wisdom that I hope to communicate in this book. Few, if any, of these nuggets are solely my insights. Most of these insights have emerged from discussions, debates, and, occasionally, heated arguments in my own company, as well as in my frequent seminars, workshops, and consulting efforts with other enterprises. I am indebted to the many, many people—from over 25 countries and 5 continents—who have contributed substantially to the basis of this book.

I am also indebted to Russ Hunt and Bill Cody—we have done much woodworking and hiking together, both in reality and metaphorically. Their numerous comments and suggestions on early drafts of this book proved invaluable. I also greatly value the insights of my editor, Mike Hays, whose comments and those he solicited from others were very helpful. I am pleased to also acknowledge the assistance of Sueann Gustin, who has long supported me in coordinating my seminars and workshops associated with the material in this book, as well as of Bonnie Sikorski, who helped me with the production of this book.

William B. Rouse
Atlanta, Georgia

1

Introduction

This book focuses on the basis of a phenomenon aptly characterized by Scottish poet Robert Burns:

The best laid schemes of mice and men
Go oft awry;
And leave us naught but grief and pain,
For promised joy.

Why do plans go awry? What is difficult about planning? How
do the answers to these questions depend on the nature of the
planning problem of interest? Given answers to these questions,
how can you decrease the "grief and pain" and increase the "joy"?

Perhaps the best place to start our discussion of these questions is to consider who experiences these difficulties. A few examples can illustrate the pervasiveness of planning problems. These
examples also serve to move us from abstract generalities to concrete reality.

PLANNING PROBLEMS

In the late 1960s, I worked for a large defense contractor. This
electronics company correctly anticipated the decline in defense
expenditures for new procurements due to the heavy costs of the
Vietnam War. Consequently, they planned to enter the commercial
marine electronics market—in particular, the market for elec-
tronic devices on pleasure boats.

As I was departing for graduate school, the company dedicated a large new building that would house their commercial marine business. A few years later, I had the opportunity to chat with former colleagues and asked them how this commercial thrust was doing. They responded, somewhat tongue in cheek, that it is very difficult to sell a $1 million depthfinder to a weekend boater!

This depthfinder, I am sure, was highly accurate and would withstand depth charges and artillery bombardment. In fact, the depthfinder would likely survive long after the boat and boater were gone. Not surprisingly, pleasure boaters did not find the benefits worth the cost.

What was the planning problem here? My guess is that the company had a plan that included projections of units sold, revenue, and costs. Further, they probably had product development and manufacturing plans. However, it is unlikely they had a plan that focused on understanding this new market *before* they engineered their product. A very important component plan for entering a new market was missing.

I frequently present seminars and lead workshops focused on new-product planning and the formulation of associated business plans. Participants in these seminars and workshops include people from a wide variety of enterprises, ranging from Fortune 500 conglomerates to very small start-up companies. All participants attend in hopes that they will learn about methods and tools they can use to create products, systems, and services that will "delight" one or more segments of the marketplace.

I am still surprised at how often the following question emerges: "We have designed and developed a new type of widget and also have an initial manufacturing process working. What markets would you suggest are the best bets for our widget?"

Invariably, I answer, "Why did you develop your widget? Who did you expect to want the benefits provided by your widget?" Typically, these questions lead to the realization that they simply had not thought about their widget in this way. They had proceeded based on intuitions about markets and focused almost solely on technical issues associated with product functionality and manufacturing processes. They had a plan, but it was woefully deficient.

Not all of an enterprise's plans are related to new products, systems, and services for the marketplace. Plans are also often created for redesign of the enterprise itself. For example, plans are formulated in order to pursue goals such as delayering, downsizing, and right-sizing—three euphemisms for shrinking enterprises in terms of the number of levels in the management hierarchy and the number of overall employees. Other examples include plans for large-scale technology infusions (e.g., automation and information systems) and plans for improving quality.

Many of these types of plans encounter substantial difficulties. As major organizational changes are implemented, productivity and morale plummet. Substantial infusions of technology create havoc. Automation, information systems, and the like, are shelved or removed. The implementation of quality programs is such that employees become quite cynical about management's commitment to the quality philosophy.

How do such best laid plans run amuck? My experience is that failed plans often suffer from a lack of considering all the "stakeholders" in the implementation of plans. Few plans are without indirect consequences in terms of changed roles, training needs, and potential periods of decreased productivity as people learn how to make the best of changes. Implementation plans should consider such indirect consequences *prior* to implementation and should involve stakeholders in determining how to deal with these consequences.

Many of the participants in my seminars and workshops come from companies that are attempting—or at least entertaining the possibility of attempting—to convert from defense markets to commercial markets. Some of these companies have plans, or at least well-articulated visions. Many companies, however, feel stuck in the status quo.

One company with which I am quite familiar has experienced a 50 percent decrease in the number of employees and is dependent on two large defense contracts for a major portion of its remaining business. When I asked them how they were dealing with this situation, they told me that they were inundating defense agencies with as many proposals as possible. I asked if they really thought this would work. The answer was, "No, but it's the only thing that we know how to do."

They said that things might get worse. Their two large contracts were with the same agency and part of a program that Congress might cancel at any time. I asked the president of this company how he was planning for this possibility. He said, "Every morning, I get up and read the newspaper to see if we are still in business."

The planning problem here, obviously, is a lack of plans. This company is so busy doing what it has always done well that its managers do not have the spare capacity to plan for alternative futures. Further, the prospects of having to make major changes seem overwhelming.

The examples thus far have dealt with the product-planning and organizational aspects of business planning. Difficulties with planning also are common for individuals. For example, thousands of middle-management positions have been eliminated in recent years, demolishing many people's plans for making it up the corporate ladder.

Typically, people in such situations search for similar positions in other enterprises. However, almost all enterprises are eliminating these types of positions. The result is that many people have to do some serious career planning. A primary difficulty lies in discovering alternative and attractive vocations, as well as in making a successful transition to a new career path.

Even for those people whose jobs have not been threatened, career paths are likely to change substantially. Many enterprises are shifting from the paradigm of control to one of collaboration. This requires employees to accept more responsibility for their job performance and for the personal development necessary to assure and improve performance.

This trend can be liberating, but also frustrating. A sequence of positions no longer assures progress up the ladder. In fact, the ladder may be slowly disappearing. What matters is contributions to achieving the enterprise's goals—not goals dictated from "on high," but goals that emerge via a collaborative process of planning which requires that all members of the team claim "ownership" of the collective plans. The result is that everyone, to an extent, becomes a planner. This can be a mixed blessing for people with no experience in planning.

UNDERLYING DIFFICULTIES

Why is the planning of products, businesses, and careers so difficult? Having helped thousands of people address problems such as described in these examples, I think that the sources of planning problems are quite straightforward. Three particular difficulties predominate.

First, people simply do not know what to do. They may know what a plan should look like, for example, in terms of format. However, they are often unsure of the nature of the thinking that goes into planning. In my planning workshops, a common question is "If I am thinking strategically, how will I know?"

People ask such questions because the overwhelming natural tendency is to focus on the concrete here and now of today's problems. Planning, particularly strategic planning, is not a natural act. In contrast, reacting to today's problems is very natural. From this perspective, it is easy to understand why people are not sure of what to do about planning and, consequently, just worry about how to deal with today's crisis, opportunity, or whatever is on today's agenda.

A second source of difficulty is time. Planning frequently takes a long time—sometimes a very long time. This is due, in part, to people's not knowing what to do. Another reason is that many planning processes are ill-structured, inadequately led, and poorly understood. As a consequence, people become frustrated spinning their wheels, often recreating wheels in the process.

The third source of planning problems—particularly frustrations with planning—is the most telling. Many planning efforts do not result in anything that the participants value and find useful. Planning is done either because it is required or out of a sense that it must be necessary. Once plans are completed, they are submitted, filed, or shelved. Life continues as it did before the planning exercise.

Put simply, people often do not know how to plan; their planning activities consume enormous amounts of time; and even when done, they often don't have anything they want. It should be no surprise that many people dread planning and resent the effort it requires. What is needed is concepts, principles, methods, and tools that make it very clear what is to be done, that do not require much time to use, and that enable creation of useful and usable plans. This book is aimed at meeting these needs.

Beyond the three general difficulties just described, there are several other special problems. One is the general resistance to change in large organizations. As organizations grow, in both public and private sectors, they tend to become institutions. An increasingly significant portion of their resources becomes devoted to preserving the institution. Change often threatens these resources, and resistance develops.

Change is also very difficult when people have to plan in an environment where top management provides little or no vision of where the enterprise is headed. While planning is often best done in a bottom-up manner, it is usually important that there be top-down leadership of the planning process. Without such leadership, much energy can be wasted and many counterproductive tangents can emerge.

Another special problem, particularly relevant today, is defense conversion. As illustrated in the earlier examples, defense companies have great difficulty transitioning to nondefense markets. Not only do they have to offer different products, systems, and services to be successful, they also have to transform their belief systems concerning customers, users, costs, technology, innovation, and so on. If they do not make this transformation, they are likely to try to sell $1 million depthfinders for $50,000 boats!

Yet another special planning problem involves enterprises operating in market environments that impose very tight constraints. For example, regulatory processes may greatly constrain what can be done and how fast it can be done. For companies whose whole business is supplying, for instance, component parts to a single, much larger company, the degrees of freedom may seem very limited.

Planning efforts can encounter particularly stubborn problems when internal stakeholders (e.g., colleagues, supervisors, and subordinates) do not support the process. In uncertain and confusing organizational environments, these stakeholders' priorities may be such that their individual interests dominate their agendas to the exclusion of enterprise-wide interests. Problems with internal stakeholders can often be more plaguing than those with external stakeholders, such as the marketplace or investors.

Thus, there are three general difficulties and a variety of special difficulties. This book elaborates these difficulties and discusses surprisingly simple concepts and principles for dealing with them. Before proceeding with these discussions, it is important that we entertain a *very* simple method for avoiding these difficulties. This simple solution is—don't plan.

VALUE OF PLANNING

To evaluate this alternative, we need to understand what planning is intended to accomplish—its "value added" within an enterprise's activities or within our own personal activities. One possibility is that planning has no value. Is planning overrated?

It can reasonably be argued that successful enterprises, and successful people, represent successes of evolution, not planning. For example, the railroad, automobile, aircraft, and computer industries all started with hundreds, if not thousands, of new companies. Over time, the fittest survived, not because they planned, but because they happened, perhaps by chance, to pick the right tactic. Similarly, great people did not plan to be great. They emerged due to a confluence of their abilities and the opportunities presented by the times. Thus, the importance of planning may be a myth!

While there is some merit to this argument, it ignores a primary reason why organizations and people plan. Recently, in a seven-day period, I helped four types of organizations with their strategic planning: (1) a Fortune 500 electronics company, (2) a government agency, (3) a nonprofit research center, and (4) a church congregation. Reflecting on these four experiences, it was clear to me that they all shared the same problem. They wanted to set priorities and allocate scarce resources (e.g., money and energy) among competing alternatives. Further, they wanted the planning groups, and the organization as a whole, to support and "buy into" the resulting plans. Put simply, they wanted plans that would enable them to proceed with consensus and confidence.

While the evidence may be meager that planning results in a better future, it is clear that people are more confident of where they are going when they have well-articulated plans with broad organizational support. Good plans enable people to be confident that current activities are consistent with the future being pursued. Due to unforeseen forces and events, good plans do not guarantee that this vision of this future will be realized. At the very least, however, good plans assure that current actions will not undermine the desired future.

As noted earlier, this book focuses on the means for understanding and overcoming planning difficulties. The remainder of this chapter discusses several themes that are woven through these discussions of concepts, principles, methods, and tools for successful planning.

CENTRAL THEMES

One theme is the value of *structured approaches for planning*. There is a myth that the best way to obtain good plans is to put a group of creative, intelligent people in a room with a blank white board and, after a day or two, they will emerge with cogent, well-articulated, and useful plans. I have participated in and seen this tried many times. Seldom do good plans result. Frequently, no plans result.

What happens in the room for the one or two days? For the first half-day or so, people raise pressing issues and often address them at very tactical levels. Toward the end of the first day, one or more participants vocalize a concern that everyone is having, "We are almost halfway through our planning session, and we do not seem to be making any progress."

Faced with this problem, the focus of the group then shifts to the problem of how to plan. They may debate and agree upon definitions of goals, strategies, plans, and so on. In one case, the group actually produced a theory of planning. Succinctly, the group often spends the rest of their time together structuring the problem of planning. When the planning session ends, the group knows much more about planning, but it has not produced any plans!

Why does this happen? It can be explained by the typical backgrounds of participants in such meetings. Managers are trained to organize and control via structure. Finance people live in very structured worlds of spreadsheet models. Engineers are trained to create structure. Scientists are trained to search for structure. Consequently, when a group of managers, finance people, engineers, and so on is given an unstructured task, there is a natural tendency to focus on structuring the task before proceeding.

By adopting structured approaches to planning, several examples of which I discuss in this book, planning groups are enabled to focus on the content of plans. All their creativity and intelligence can be used to formulate useful and usable plans. Such approaches not only enable you to know what you are doing, but if the approaches are well designed, they also enable you to produce plans very quickly.

While structure can greatly facilitate planning, it is not a panacea. One difficulty that structured approaches often make painfully obvious is the lack of an appropriate representation or formulation of the planning problem being addressed. Many of the companies with whom I work are focused on how to design, develop, manufacture, market, sell, and service new products. They want help in formulating plans to accomplish these goals.

The difficulty is that these are often the wrong goals. The real planning problem concerns innovating in the marketplace—creating change in terms of demands for new or different products. Design, development, and the like, are the means to this end, not the end in themselves.

People often have difficulty dealing with this issue. They have a natural tendency to want to "get on with it" and employ the structured methodology to formulate a plan for getting their new widget into the market as quickly as possible. Further, they often have already decided exactly what the widget will be like. Thus, it is not at all appealing to consider "backing up" and making sure that they know what will be required to innovate in the markets of interest.

The essence of this problem is that people have often implicitly committed themselves to a particular representation of the planning problem. This representation needs to be made explicit and, if necessary, modified before planning proceeds too far. Otherwise, there is a substantial risk that they will create an excellent plan—an excellent solution—for the wrong problem.

Thus, beyond structured approaches to planning, there is also the need for a means of freeing the planning process from implicit and unquestioned assumptions. A second theme throughout this book deals with one means for accomplishing this. This theme concerns *lateral thinking via metaphors*.

We all tend to get stuck in the concrete, everyday reality of our tasks, jobs, and businesses. Often the meanings and usage of words become, in effect, standardized, and we find new concepts difficult to communicate. In such situations, we may resort to analogies or metaphors. For example, we might attempt to explain organizational communication problems in terms of the ways that members of a basketball team communicate. As another illustration, we might use the metaphor of a factory to explain how a new training center will "produce" trained personnel.

Metaphorical thinking and communication are inevitable. We frequently have to resort to common, well-understood contexts to explain phenomena ranging from quantum physics to organizational cultures. In this way, we enable others to understand the essence of something without all the messy details that get in the way of understanding. By talking to people in terms of contexts other than those of their own tasks and jobs, we also enable them to escape the very natural tendency to get bogged down in details. As a result, people are able to move laterally, out of their normal linear thinking, and see things in different ways.

In this book, I discuss three primary metaphors. Woodworking, hiking, and discovery are used to facilitate thinking about the planning of products, businesses, and life, respectively. The discussion of these metaphors focuses on understanding a variety of simple planning principles as they apply to woodworking, hiking, and discovery. These principles are then generalized in the contexts of product, business, and life planning.

Woodworking, in general, and designing and manufacturing furniture, in particular, serve as a metaphor for all product planning. Furniture is an easily understood, concrete product whose design and manufacture involve all the issues, albeit often in simplified form, that surround the design and manufacture of all products and systems. Of particular importance, furniture design and manufacture is a domain that is readily understood by a wide range of people. Thus, this metaphor provides a good context within which to initially explain the concepts and principles of product planning.

Hiking is a metaphor for all business planning. Hiking involves a journey with clear long-term goals, a variety of milestones, and a team of people who must work together to succeed. The parallels with business planning are quite clear, although hiking is much simpler and an easier domain within which to first illustrate the concepts and principles of business planning advanced in this book.

Discovery is a metaphor for life planning. The reason for choosing this metaphor is that the process of discovery can be planned, but the particular things discovered cannot. Life planning is similar. This metaphor focuses first on "external" discovery in other cultures and societies. This discussion then provides a basis for subsequently focusing on the "internal" discovery of life planning.

Using these three metaphors, we visit sawmills, mountaintops, and dusty bazaars on our journey toward understanding. These easy-to-explain contexts introduce and illustrate a variety of simple planning principles. Subsequently, these principles are generalized to the reality of planning products, businesses, and lives.

A third theme in this book concerns *process*. Planning is a process that yields products—plans. My experience is that good processes yield good products. For this reason, much of the discussion in this book concerns process.

Four process issues are emphasized. The first is "vision," or imagining alternative futures and their consequences. Imagining alternative futures is central to moving beyond the status quo. Other than for preserving traditions, plans that simply rationalize the status quo are seldom of much value. However, to move beyond the status quo in an intentional manner, we must entertain change, often substantial change.

This can be very challenging. The status quo is usually quite compelling. The overwhelmingly natural tendency is to do today what we did yesterday. It is also natural to think today as we thought yesterday. Fortunately, metaphorical thinking can break these bonds.

Another issue is "choice," or choosing among and committing to alternative futures. Choice and commitment are the ultimate outcomes of planning. Indeed, avoidance of making choices and committing to action is often a prime reason that planning fails. Alternative futures are wistfully considered, but almost without realizing it, life happens and best laid plans have remained unused on the shelf.

A third issue is time. Planning inherently involves the future, which implies the passage of time. Thus, planning must deal with time in terms of what changes are possible over what time scale, as well as what processes inextricably evolve regardless of decisions made or not made. Planning also is concerned with the relative value of outcomes at different points in time.

Planning, and the plans that result, often concerns the allocation of time. In particular, allocation of the time and attention of key people is a central concern. While organizations and individuals can accumulate more and more money and tangible assets, time is not similarly expandable. Regardless of your creativity, intelligence, and commitment, you are limited to 24 hours per day.

This is particularly important in life planning. Your most precious resource is your time. How you allocate this resource speaks volumes about who you are and what is important to you. Consequently, the allocation of time should be an intentional act.

A fourth issue related to the process theme concerns "relationships"; these necessarily involve the stakeholders, animate and inanimate, in any particular planning effort. Relationships are central to all types of planning in that consideration must be given to other people and to the environment within which planning takes place. While relationships such as these can be viewed as constraints within which plans must fit, I have found that both animate and inanimate relationships are often the primary means to successful planning and implementation.

Animate relationships concern other people, as well as other species in the environment. Inanimate relationships involve tools, trails, and cultures. To the extent that animate and inanimate relationships involve collaboration, rather than control, I have found that planning and implementation of the resulting plans can be greatly facilitated.

The distinction between control and collaboration is very important and emerges repeatedly throughout this book. Many of us have a tendency to want to control activities and events—to make things happen. This may be due to a need for power. However, at least as important is the need to be confident that things will happen.

Collaboration involves relinquishing, or at least distributing, control. Rather than imposing our will on people and things, we confidently let people and things do their jobs and play their roles. While we may mentor and coach, we don't command and control.

For most people and organizations, the shift from control to collaboration represents a paradigm change. Such changes relate to the fourth theme woven throughout this book—*transformation and growth*. Much of planning, and most good planning, is concerned with change. This change might be a reluctant response to external pressures. Alternatively, change can be the means whereby products, organizations, and people are transformed and, consequently, grow to become new.

To a great extent, the primary emphasis of this book concerns the role of planning in transformation and growth. While planning cannot guarantee desirable changes, appropriate planning processes and tools can create an environment that is open to change. In fact, a variety of simple planning concepts can make change much easier than you might expect.

Enabling transformation and growth requires that we overcome many people's resistance to change. Our society, and especially our economy, is coming to recognize change as a natural state rather than an aberration. Nevertheless, many people are having a very difficult time adopting this perspective.

Such difficulties can be overcome, at least in part, by understanding the typical course of change. There is a fairly natural but often rocky process whereby the old way of doing things "dies" and the new way matures. It can be particularly anguishing if the old way has to be maintained in parallel with the new way while the new way slowly matures. This is true for product lines, businesses, and careers. Fortunately, understanding and anticipating this process can substantially lower stress levels while experiencing it.

OVERVIEW

The questions, themes, issues, and metaphors elaborated in this introductory chapter are pursued in this book in the context of three types of planning problems. The first type of problem discussed is *product planning*. This problem is concerned with conceptualizing, designing, developing, manufacturing, marketing, selling, and supporting new products, systems, and services. Building on the metaphor of woodworking, a general set of concepts and principles for product planning is presented and illustrated with a variety of vignettes.

The second type of problem considered is *business planning*. This type of problem is concerned with the same types of activities as product planning, except the object of these activities is an enterprise's processes rather than its products. Beyond the planning of processes, business planning is also concerned with the organization and control of these processes. Using the metaphor of hiking as a starting point, concepts and principles for business planning are discussed in the context of numerous vignettes related to how these ideas have been successfully employed.

The third type of problem of interest is *life planning*. Problems of this type are concerned with expectations, aspirations, and choices about education, vocations, avocations, and life issues in general. While you usually do not plan your life with the same degree of rigor as may be possible for products and businesses, many of the concepts and principles discussed in this book apply across all three of these planning problems. The metaphor of discovery is used as a point of departure for applying these ideas to several issues that are central to our lives.

Summarizing, this book is concerned with planning products, businesses, and life in general. My overall goal is to introduce you to a variety of simple yet compelling principles for planning. These principles are illustrated in the context of numerous stories and vignettes. Many are drawn from experiences with my company's software products and systems, as well as from our overall business planning. Many more, however, are drawn from experiences helping a wide range of enterprises produce better plans.

2

Woodworking

Woodworking is a process whereby you and the wood uncover and create what each other will become.

To begin our discussions of product planning, we consider a very straightforward product-planning domain—woodworking. This is a good place to start because furniture is a concrete product whose design and manufacture involve all the fundamental issues, albeit often in simplified form, that surround the design and manufacture of all products and systems. In this way, designing and manufacturing furniture can provide many insights into planning in general. This chapter focuses on the specifics of woodworking. The next chapter generalizes the conclusions of this chapter to all product planning.

WOODWORKING AS A PROCESS

Woodworking can be viewed as a process that includes several steps or phases. This process begins by defining a need, and then creating or selecting a design. Often, the creation of a design involves modifying a previous design. Modifications might include changes of dimensions (e.g., table width or length), adding and/or deleting features (e.g., number of drawers), changes of methods for joining materials (e.g., adding dovetail joints), or changes of materials and/or finishes.

Some designs start from scratch. For example, a few years ago, I designed and built two large flower tables for our deck. The design of these tables was driven by the size of cedar pieces left over from adding a trellis roof to our deck. The dimensions and style of these tables were determined by what I could imagine emerging from the scrap pile. Nevertheless, both tables had four legs, were rectangular in shape, and were put together with pretty standard joints. Thus, the resulting tables do not look particularly unique.

My guess is that most products are like this. They have a few features that are new and perhaps unique, but most aspects of products are borrowed from other products. For example, the software products and systems produced by my company employ many standard features in, for instance, the human-computer interface. In fact, there is considerable pressure from the marketplace to standardize the interface to make products and systems easier to use.

Given a design, the next step of woodworking involves planning fabrication. This includes designing components and the pieces to be cut that will form components or be assembled to form components. Methods of joining pieces and components are also designed. Requirements for materials, finishes, and hardware are determined.

Decisions made in this step have important downstream implications. The difficulty and time required to manufacture the furniture are determined by the design of its pieces, components, joints, and assembly methods. I have often needed to produce 3, 6, or 12 of the same piece in parallel. This may involve making the same cut 24 or 48 times. By simplifying designs and avoiding difficult cuts, a minute or so may be saved per cut. Several instances of such simplifications can save an hour or two per piece.

Selection of materials can also have a big impact. If my only concern was cost, I would choose pine. If the dominant concern was ease of manufacturing, I would pick basswood. However, I often choose mahogany because I find the grain of this wood very appealing, particularly after several coats of oil.

Obtaining materials can also be an issue. For pine, I usually go to the local supply house. For other woods, however, I often go to a sawmill about 20 miles north of where I live. Trips to this sprawling cluster of ramshackle buildings are a treat for me. The buzzing noises and aromatic smells are wonderful.

At this sawmill, you pick your own wood, piece by piece. For basswood, I usually look at about 2 pieces for each one piece I select. For mahogany, I inspect 5 to 10 pieces per piece selected. For cherry, it might be 10 to 20.

Inspection involves making sure that pieces have sufficient width and are not cracked or split. The size and integrity of knots are also important. Knots can be attractive if they are not too large and do not start to separate from the rest of the wood.

It also is useful to imagine how each board will be cut, not exactly but very loosely, relative to your manufacturing plan. Boards with too many knots may not be usable. Boards with sweeping grain patterns may be perfect for table tops or bureau sides.

I always leave the sawmill with a sense of excitement. Part of this is due to the enjoyment of being there. More compelling, however, is the sense that my carefully selected stack of wood will soon start to become the end tables or bureau that I recently completed designing or redesigning. The desire to physically manifest your product concept is an important force in product planning.

The next step in woodworking concerns fabricating the design or, in other words, executing the manufacturing plan. Viewed simply, this step involves cutting all the pieces and putting them together. This view is, however, much too simple.

Much of the work of cutting involves getting set up to cut. Often, this includes only adjusting blade heights, moving guide fences, and so on. However, setup is more complicated when accuracy is very important (i.e., because things have to fit together snugly) and/or repeatability is critical (i.e., because component pieces have to be interchangeable).

When accuracy and/or repeatability is central, it is common to design jigs that enable rapid production of pieces that satisfy these requirements. Often the design, fabrication, and testing of a jig requires longer than using it to produce the desired pieces. In one instance, it took me four hours to build and test a jig for cutting tapered legs and only one-half hour to actually cut the four legs for the table that I was building. Fortunately, that jig has been used to build four other tables since its original use.

Another time-consuming element of setup can be producing test pieces. This involves using scrap wood to create test pieces or components to assure that the setup, perhaps including jigs, is right. This is important to assure that joints are snug, drawers can be closed and opened, and so on.

Occasionally, setup can be minimized. Not long ago, I designed a cutaway dollhouse that hangs on the wall to exhibit the furnishing of its rooms. I needed to produce three of these houses in one evening. Fortunately, they did not have to be identical. This allowed me to "prototype" each one, cutting joints free-hand on the table saw and adjusting angles, depths, and so forth, as a prototype evolved. This was quick, but pieces were not interchangeable and many joints were not snug. Wallpaper and other finishes covered any imperfections.

Were I to need to produce such dollhouses again, I would use one of these prototypes as a starting point. I would then design jigs that enable rapid production of as many identical dollhouses as are wanted. The creation of such jigs would probably take longer than it took to create the original prototypes. However, all future dollhouses would be produced much faster and would be much better dollhouses.

Fabrication also involves assembly and bonding. Most bonding uses wood glue and only occasionally screws and nails. In most cases, you get only one chance—disassembling a glued bond usually damages the pieces and they cannot be used again.

To avoid this, assembly is first done "dry." The assembled components are checked for alignment and squareness. If these requirements are inherently satisfied by the squareness and tightness of joints, then assembly is straightforward. Compensating for irregular pieces or loose joints can be very time consuming.

Several of the examples just noted illustrate an important principle. Time spent upstream in the woodworking process usually saves time downstream *and* yields a better product. Thus, attempting to save time upstream seldom yields an overall savings. In fact, the downstream costs may far exceed any upstream savings. Whether you are designing furniture, computer software, or airplanes, good planning provides ample payback.

Assembly is usually one of the "joys" of woodworking. Prior to assembly, you have only pieces of wood. Millwork and other processes may have yielded interesting and pleasing shapes. However, the act of putting it together is usually more satisfying. Before you had only wood, but now you have a piece of furniture, or at least an emerging piece of furniture.

Fabrication also includes sanding and finishing. Sanding can often be done faster and better prior to assembly, since individual pieces are often flat and more easily accessible. The process of sanding requires patience as you switch from heavier-duty to lighter sanders and from coarser- to finer-grit sandpapers.

Finishing may involve the use of paints, varnishes, stains, or oils. My preference is oil. I like to see the real wood, with the grains, knots, and occasional imperfections. It is also interesting to see how woods darken as an oil finish ages. Overall, there is a type of sensuality to a hand-rubbed oil finish on beautiful woods such as mahogany or cherry.

The final step of woodworking involves "servicing" the product. This includes protecting and enhancing the finish. Repairs may occasionally be necessary. Design modifications may also be required as the user's needs change. Perhaps, if you are very good and very lucky, someone may eventually value your creation as an antique and refinish it with loving care.

DECIDING WHAT TO BUILD

Pursuit of all the above steps or phases depends on being able to answer a very basic question in woodworking: "What to build?" Answering this question requires consideration of several issues. These issues are the same regardless of the product you are designing.

Stakeholders

The first issue concerns the needs and desires of potential users and customers for your furniture. Users and customers are central stakeholders in your woodworking efforts. There often are other stakeholders. For example, if furniture is to be used in other than private homes (e.g., in businesses, schools, and churches), there may be stakeholders such as facility caretakers/maintainers and perhaps those who regulate product safety.

The concept of stakeholders is central to the approach to product planning discussed in this book. A primary tenet of this approach is consideration for and balancing of the concerns, values, and perceptions of all stakeholders in a design effort. Put simply, if all stakeholders perceive that a product provides the benefits they seek at an acceptable cost, the product will be a success.

This conclusion dictates that you identify all the stakeholders and then find out what is important to them. The product design problem is thereby framed as one of synthesizing a concept that "delights" all the stakeholders. A straightforward method for framing design problems in this way is discussed in Chapter 3.

Who are the typical stakeholders in furniture design? As long as we limit our "market" to homes, the answer is clearly customers and users. Further, in most but not all cases, the customer is the user, or at least one of the users.

Stakeholders' Needs and Desires

Thus, our design problem is very much simplified. What types and quality of furniture are needed and desired by our customers and users? My guess is that most people want furniture that is aesthetically pleasing, functional, durable, and inexpensive. Each of these attributes influences certain design choices.

First, consider cost. The price of a piece of furniture is dictated by the cost of creating the furniture, the cost of getting someone to buy it, and the profits made by the manufacturer, distributor, furniture store, and so forth. From a design point of view, the key is the cost of creating the furniture. This cost includes the costs of investments in facilities and tools as well as the costs of materials, hardware, and labor. Ideally, you would like to use the fewest tools, cheapest materials, and as little labor as possible.

These objectives might be achieved by creating a design that requires only straight cuts, involves very simple joints, uses only pine, and can be built in a few minutes. This minimizes investment in tools and jigs, minimizes costs of materials, and involves only a few dollars of labor. Unfortunately, such a strategy may severely compromise the other attributes of interest to customers and users.

For example, durability may require more complicated joints—for instance, mortise and tenon joints rather than butt joints. This is likely to necessitate special jigs to assure the fit of joints as well as the interchangeability of pieces. This, in turn, will require an investment of time in building and testing these jigs. It may also result in more setup time when producing these joints.

Durability may also dictate using a wood other than pine. Perhaps oak or teak may be needed to assure, for example, that the garden benches you are creating will last in the hot sun and damp rains. These woods are more expensive and a bit more time consuming to use. Cutting these woods is not like zipping through butter, such as cutting pine or basswood can be. Blades and bits also wear out more quickly. Thus, tool costs may increase.

Functionality requirements also tend to complicate design and production. It is much easier to make a table, say a vanity, without drawers. By including drawers, manufacturing time is substantially increased, materials costs increase somewhat, and additional tools and jigs may be needed. However, if you do not include drawers in your design, selling your vanity may be difficult.

A very important attribute concerns aesthetics, or the style of furniture. Having delved into this topic a bit, I can report that there are many more styles of furniture than you might imagine. Most styles from past periods are only of interest to collectors now—we have a few pieces that are interesting to look at but awful to sit in or use.

I tend to build two styles. One is the basic Shaker style, with long tapered legs and simple straight lines. I also like to build pieces that look more classic, with much millwork and intricate joinery. There are, of course, many other styles, such as Scandinavian and Spanish/Southwestern, that I have yet to try.

A key element of aesthetics for me is the choice of wood. As I noted earlier, I like to use oil finishes rather than stains, varnishes, or paints. Thus, the character of the wood is very important. Not surprisingly, using high-quality, interesting hardwoods results in higher materials costs. Such woods also tend to require more time for planning (e.g., to reduce waste) and more time for production (e.g., to avoid waste).

Overall, it is easy to see that a variety of tradeoffs emerges. Increased durability and functionality tend to increase costs. Increased aesthetic appeal tends to increase costs. A portion of these increases is due to greater materials costs. A much greater portion, in my experience, is due to increased time for planning and production. Further, if you skimp on planning time, the usual result is increases in production time that are much greater than the savings in planning.

Where does this leave us in terms of trying to delight our stakeholders? Clearly, you need a thorough understanding of how stakeholders view the tradeoffs just outlined in order to assure that you will be creating furniture people want at a price that you can charge in order to make a reasonable living. Even if you do not sell the furniture you design and build, as I usually don't, you still have to be concerned with what will please people and meet their needs, from both practical and aesthetic perspectives.

Let's assume, for the sake of argument, that you have a good understanding of what stakeholders need and want. It would seem that you are all set—start designing and building. My guess, however, is that those customers and users you queried may have many more needs and wants than you can satisfy. Which should you choose to try to satisfy?

Competencies and Resources

This leads to an issue of competencies and resources. What are your woodworking strengths? What experiences can you draw on? Furniture designs that involve using your strengths and experiences are much easier to build and lead to a higher-quality product more quickly.

These questions dictate that you understand your strengths and weaknesses. When building designs that I have not previously built, I try to include features that involve well-honed skills (e.g., certain types of millwork) and at least one feature where my experience is minimal. For example, a recent project building a chest of drawers involved many dovetail joints with which I had limited experience.

This strategy emphasizes drawing on strengths and overcoming at least one weakness. In choosing which weakness to focus on—and the set is large—I try to choose an area that is central to other woodworking efforts that I anticipate pursuing. Of course, most of my weaknesses will inevitably never get any attention, which is a comfort in itself.

A recent experience showed me that I tend to take many competencies for granted. One of these is vision. My first experience with bifocal glasses made this clear. I was cutting pieces on the band saw and, depending on the angle of my head, the pencil lines on the wood would either appear or disappear.

At first I was confused and tried adjusting the lighting, which did not help at all. Then I noticed that the angle of my head seemed to have an effect. Finally, it dawned on me that I was wearing my new bifocals for the first time while woodworking. I immediately knew which angles of my head were necessary to have consistent vision.

While it may sound silly, I paused for a moment and thought about how important a basic competency such as vision is to my avocation of woodworking. It also struck me, metaphorical thinker that I am, how important one's point of view can be. From the wrong perspective, my cutting task could not be done. Looking from another angle, however, made the task simple. I wonder how often this phenomenon affects us in many things we do? This question emerges again in Chapters 6 and 7.

Beyond competencies, you also should consider resources. What tools and raw materials are available or obtainable? What jigs are on hand or can be created?

Your tools and jigs, and of course your workshop, reflect your capital investments in woodworking. Usually you attempt to take advantage of investments to assure that they yield acceptable returns. Thus, you should purchase tools and create jigs that have future uses. These become elements of the resources that influence what you choose to build.

The availability and costs of materials, hardware, and so forth, also have an influence. Having materials on hand—perhaps left in inventory from past projects—may make choices quite straightforward. It also may be easy to choose to avoid creating furniture that requires exotic and expensive woods that may take considerable time to acquire.

Overall, the issue of competencies and resources influences the choice of what to build in terms of your assessment of what is reasonable to assume you can accomplish. If many new skills, as well as new resources, are necessary for success, you may want to choose a different type of furniture to build. In contrast, if a design requires only well-honed skills and readily available resources, your woodworking effort may yield little personal growth. This tradeoff is relatively clear.

Aspirations and Expectations

To an extent, this tradeoff can be resolved by addressing another issue that underlies the question of what to build. This issue concerns the aspirations and expectations of a very central stakeholder—you. Do you aspire to produce potential heirlooms or sturdy backyard furniture? Both may be wanted by your likely customers and users. However, which do you want to produce?

I believe that product planning should be market driven—in other words, driven by stakeholders' concerns, values, and perceptions. However, I also believe that the choice of which plan to implement should be highly influenced by your aspirations. If you have a "fire in the belly" desire to build certain types of furniture *and* your product plans show that your vision makes sense, then do it!

The likely success of a plan is highly related to the extent of commitment and ownership that key people feel toward the plan. Without commitment and ownership, plans that would otherwise be judged as good may end with a whimper. For these reasons, what you want to do should be a compelling force.

The other side of aspirations is expectations. What do you expect you will be able to accomplish? What are the likely consequences of these accomplishments? Are these consequences desirable, or at least acceptable? Are your aspirations and expectations compatible?

The question of what furniture to build involves, on the surface, a complex set of tradeoffs among potential needs and wants in terms of attributes such as aesthetics, functionality, durability, and price. Once these tradeoffs are framed, it is often the case, with furniture or other products, that there are many possibilities for delighting customers, users, and other stakeholders. The final choice should be strongly influenced by the needs and wants of those who are going to have to invest themselves in creating the product and in assuring that the needs and wants of the marketplace are satisfied.

DECIDING HOW TO BUILD IT

Beyond the question of what to build, there is the question of how to build it. This question shifts the emphasis from products to processes. Concerns now focus on planning fabrication, as well as on the actual fabrication of products.

Manufacturability

Of central importance to the design of most products is manufacturability. It is quite possible for the design of a piece of furniture to require excessive material and substantially excessive production time, without providing any incremental value to customers. These consequences are due almost solely to lack of consideration of the difficulty—and hence the resources required—for manufacturing. However, with a bit of forethought substantial savings can be realized.

Consider a very simple example. Every spring for the past five or six years, my daughter has prevailed upon me to help her with year-end gifts for her school teachers. This has resulted in a family "stool factory." I design and build pine foot stools, my daughter creates a "teacher-centered" painting on each stool—depicting, for example, each teacher's hobbies—and my wife puts a protective finish on each stool.

The first year, we did 1 or 2 stools. Then, we built 3. The year before last, our output was 6. This year we built 12. I should note that the "market" drove these production demands—as children get older, they have more teachers!

As manager of stool design and production, my problem has typically been one of delivering 6 or 12 stools in response to an "order" that usually comes at the last minute—unfortunately, customers never seem to learn! In order to be responsive, I have redesigned my stools each year. I have modified dimensions to improve functionality from teachers' points of view. I have added various fancy cuts and millwork flourishes to improve the "image" of my stools.

Unfortunately, all of these additions have tended to increase production time. This past year, with an urgent order for 12 stools in hand, I decided to see if I could decrease production time without compromising quality and image. In fact, this focus was driven by the need to produce the 12 stools in one day!

Such a rush order usually results in panic. Normally, I would have pulled out last year's drawings and started cutting. However, a fairly brief analysis led to a few interesting conclusions.

- Because of the size and pricing of available materials, I could increase the size of the stools at *no* increased materials costs or time.

- Because of experience with certain types of millwork, I could add a few "fancy" features with almost *no* setup costs.

- Two of the curved millwork features of last year's stools were *very* time consuming but could be replaced by straight, but still appealing features.

These observations led to redesign of our stools. This redesign included the design and fabrication of a jig for stool end pieces that required one hour to create, but that then produced 24 stool ends in 15 minutes. In the end, after much reflection and redesign, the customer had 12 delightful stools within one day!

What did I learn from this experience? The overwhelming answer is that numerous features of these stools were designed based on very ambiguous aesthetic criteria. Once I realized that I needed to "ship" my customer 12 pieces of furniture in one day, I focused on assuring that appealing aesthetic features were also easily manufacturable.

It is very easy to generalize this lesson. Manufacturing and production functions are stakeholders in the success of product planning. You should look at the problem from their points of view —perhaps by walking in their shoes. Not surprisingly, this experience suddenly makes the problem compelling—having to build furniture yourself is substantially different from telling other people what to build.

Materials Planning

Another element of process planning is materials planning. I build pine stools for my daughter—my customer. Why not build mahogany or rosewood stools? The answer is simple. Mahogany or rosewood is too expensive relative to customers' expectations.

Materials planning involves two basic issues—which materials and how much? While I tend to like the finer hardwoods, does this make sense for customers? My guess is that the expected quality of woods relates to purpose or function. People do not expect, or know how to value, a rosewood stool. Similarly, most people do not expect a pine highboy.

Thus, the choice of materials depends substantially on what you are building. In contrast, the efficiency with which materials are used depends on your design. Appropriate design can take advantage of available materials while also minimizing waste. For example, I created bigger stools because I had no choice but to procure longer boards—customers got more value while I spent no more on materials.

Resolution of most of the process issues discussed thus far depends on the lot size being manufactured. It seldom makes sense to invest in manufacturing plans, as well as the design and fabrication of jigs, for products or systems where only a single copy will be produced. However, if the planning horizon includes producing many copies of the design of interest—a production run of tens or hundreds or more—planning can easily be the difference between profit and despair. Planning for manufacturability and materials utilization is often central to success.

Unfortunately, the time horizon is not always clear. We tend to focus solely on the next one out. Consequently, it never seems worth it to improve process effectiveness and efficiency. In order to lengthen your time horizon, you need a good business plan. This topic is discussed in Chapters 4 and 5.

Tools and Jigs

The manufacturing of most products can be facilitated by the use of appropriate tools and jigs. The design of products, therefore, should take into account the roles of tools and jigs in creating high-quality, low-cost products. This principle is illustrated for furniture in this chapter and generalized in the next chapter.

As noted earlier, two other concerns in planning manufacturing are accuracy and repeatability of cuts. Accuracy is necessary if pieces and components are to fit together snugly, not leaving, for example, gaps in mitered corners. A very important element of accuracy is the quality of tools. I have a professional table saw that scores well on accuracy, but a hobbyist band saw that often presents accuracy problems.

Another aspect of accuracy concerns manual positioning and holding of pieces for cutting. It is very difficult to position and hold pieces manually so that you consistently achieve the same accuracy. As a consequence, pieces often do not match perfectly. This can be a relatively minor problem for a single piece, but very problematic when two pieces have to fit together.

This problem also relates to the issue of repeatability. Most furniture designs require multiple copies of the same pieces and components. For example, tables usually have four identical legs, and bureaus have four or five identical drawers. When you are making multiple copies of a stool, table, or bureau, there may be tens or hundreds of the exact same piece.

The issue of repeatability concerns assuring that each piece is exactly the same, relative to acceptable tolerances. In part, this enables good fits. At least as important, however, is the need for pieces to be interchangeable. If pieces are not interchangeable, assembly can be a major problem, and you are likely to have to carefully match pieces to assure, for example, that drawers fit.

Consequently, drawers may not be interchangeable. Thus, you have to keep track of which drawer goes where.

Reconsider the stool example. The 12 stools required 24 stool ends. Because these stool ends were all identical, any two ends could be assembled with a top and two side pieces and yield a stool that was not tippy on the floor. However, if ends were not identical, assembly would potentially involve considering all possible pairs of two ends—there are 276 possibilities. Further, once the best pairings were identified, each pair would have to be tracked through sanding and initial finishing prior to final assembly. Clearly, repeatability is important.

Quality tools can help with repeatability. Design also has a substantial impact. Cuts that present difficulty for available tools should be avoided. Cuts that can be accomplished only via manual positioning and holding should be avoided. Of most importance, particularly as lot size increases, is planning and designing pieces so that jigs can be used to assure the accuracy and repeatability of cuts.

Jigs are specialized tools that position and hold materials to allow accurate and repeatable cuts. There are generalized methods for positioning and holding materials, examples being fences and miter gauges on table saws. However, these methods are mainly for straight cuts; for more complicated cuts, these general methods are of limited help.

For instance, as noted in an earlier example, cutting tapered table legs was greatly assisted by a jig that holds the leg blank (i.e., nontapered piece of stock) at the correct angle for cutting each of its four sides. Once I completed—and tested—this jig, it was very easy to quickly produce 16 cuts (4 sides times 4 legs) that were identical.

Another example is the aforementioned jig that I created for cutting stool ends from pine blanks. The jig both held the stock and guided the saber saw for the angled cuts of the leg pattern in each stool end. As indicated earlier, I first had to redesign the stool to enable creation of this jig. It then took an hour or so to build and test this jig. Finally, 48 identical cuts (2 legs times 2 ends times 12 stools) were accomplished in a few minutes.

In some situations, it is possible to design somewhat flexible jigs. A good example is a panel cutter. It is difficult to maintain squareness when cutting large pieces on a table saw using only the fence. With the miter gauges normally furnished with table saws, it is virtually impossible to squarely cut large pieces.

A panel cutter is a wooden frame—usually a piece of plywood perhaps 24 in. by 36 in.—with an attached fence. This frame rides on top of the saw table, guided by a piece of hardwood that is attached to the bottom of the frame and fits into the groove in the saw table. Using a panel cutter, large pieces up to 30 in. by perhaps 96 in. can be positioned and held squarely as they move through the saw. This jig is very versatile in that no changes have to be made to accommodate a wide variety of sizes of pieces.

The leg-tapering jig just noted also has a degree of flexibility. By moving only one piece of the jig, legs of different lengths can be created. Thus, to an extent, this jig gives you a somewhat generic leg-making capability.

In contrast, the jig for making stool ends has absolutely no flexibility. Every blank that is inserted must be the same size. Only one type of stool end can result. Fortunately, when you want this type of stool end, it enables exactly what is needed—speed, accuracy, and repeatability.

Generalized tools and specialized jigs have a very big impact on the manufacturability of a piece of furniture. When planning for manufacturing, you should consider what can be accomplished with available tools and jigs, as well as how designs might be modified to enable new jigs. While this planning and jig building obviously adds time to the front end of manufacturing, it can provide very substantial payoffs at the back end, both in terms of cutting and assembly.

As noted earlier, tools and jigs play an important role in the design and manufacturing of most types of products. In the next chapter, this concept is elaborated and illustrated in the context of software products.

Prototypes

Once the manufacturing plan is complete, it is time to start fabrication. While this phase inherently starts with cutting pieces, seldom do you just cut the pieces, assemble them, add finish, and deliver. Initial cutting and assembly often involves much proto-typing. Once setup has been completed, one or more pieces are cut from scrap and measured and compared. Some dry assembly may be done to assure that the fabrication plan will work. Occasionally, a complete prototype is built—out of pine, for instance—prior to starting to cut expensive hardwoods.

I almost always prototype joints, millwork, and tapers—except for tapered legs where my well-used tapering jig can be employed. Joints need to be prototyped because small errors can lead to mortise and tenon joints, for example, being too loose or too tight. Without prototyping, a whole set of mitered joints may have slight, but visible, gaps.

Millwork is usually created on the router table. Fancy scrolled edges for stool tops and tabletops are among the types of milling that I do. Moldings for panels on bureaus are another example. I almost always prototype a first copy using pine scrap to assure that the setup is correct and my skills are intact.

Typically, prototypes are discarded or put on the "trophy" shelf, up high out of the way. I mentioned the instance of the doll-houses earlier where the evolving prototypes were the end prod-ucts. No two dollhouses were identical. In fact, each successive dollhouse was a bit better. If I were to decide to produce doll-houses on a regular basis, in lot sizes such that accuracy and interchangeability would become important issues, prototypes would become means rather than ends.

Prototypes serve important roles in product design in gen-eral. In the next chapter, a variety of uses for prototypes is dis-cussed. Further, a case study is used to illustrate the use of an evolving set of prototypes to gain a better understanding of stake-holders' needs and desires.

Lessons Learned

An important element of expertise in any domain is the accu-mulation of lessons learned via successes, failures, and various types of setbacks. Many of these lessons are very context specific, as illustrated by several of the following examples. However, a few of these lessons are broadly applicable.

A classical issue in manufacturing concerns cutting speeds. The speeds at which materials can be cut depends on the depth of the cut, as well as the type of material. For thick pieces, cutting must be slower to avoid overloading saws—and tripping circuit breakers. For millwork where much material is to be removed, cutting may have to be done in multiple passes.

Cutting slower can create its own set of problems. I have found that slowly cutting hardwoods, in particular, tends to result in burn marks on the wood. I first encountered this problem several years ago when I was finally able to afford more expensive woods. My natural reaction to seeing the burns on my lovely hardwoods was to cut even slower, which did not improve the situation at all. It struck me that perhaps I should move the wood faster to give the blade less opportunity to burn at any particular point in the cut. I tried it. The burning stopped.

Cutting faster solved the burning problem, but I then faced the depth-of-cut tradeoff. The obvious answer, especially for millwork, was to use multiple fast passes to remove a relatively thin layer of material with each pass. I now can readily produce high-quality milled hardwood, having made it through the learning curve just described.

Another interesting issue when cutting concerns whether the tool should be fixed and the piece moved, or vice versa. For table saws that usually weigh many hundreds of pounds, the answer is obvious. However, tools such as skill saws, saber saws, and routers are relatively light and portable.

A simple rule of thumb is to always move the lighter and/or less awkward piece. Thus, for example, cutting full sheets of plywood with a skill saw is usually a better idea than trying to keep the sheets correctly oriented as they pass through a table saw. Similarly, using a router table to edge small tabletops—by moving them through upside down—may work better than trying to position and hold such tops while moving the portable router over them.

Rules of thumb such as outlined in the last few paragraphs can make many aspects of woodworking much easier. However, frustration can still be frequent. Bad cuts happen—which I can imagine as a woodworkers' bumper sticker. The key is to transform potentially frustrating results into opportunities to learn.

One lesson learned—usually very quickly—is the value of test cuts with scrap pieces. A lesson that was much slower in coming, at least for me, is the importance of calmly tracking down the sources of systematic problems. For example, not too long ago, I had a problem with poor fits of mitered joints on the base of a bureau. I kept checking the setup, but the test cuts were not accurate or consistent.

My first hunch was an overall calibration problem. However, I reasoned that miscalibration would produce inaccuracies that were consistent, that is, always off in the same way. I finally homed in on the source of the inconsistency—me! I was not holding pieces sufficiently tight to keep the cutting forces from slightly and inconsistently causing pieces to slip. A jig was needed to rectify this problem.

Calmness in the face of bad results is, I think, a learned skill. Similarly, focusing on learning something from bad results is also a learned skill. There is yet another important skill that is best illustrated by an example.

A couple of years ago, I designed and built two mahogany end tables based on a Shaker design including tapered legs. To create the legs, I glued together two pieces of 3/4-in. mahogany stock to form leg blanks. I then used my tapering jig to cut the legs, all of which had barely visible seams on two opposing sides due to having been created from two pieces of wood.

When the tables were completed, including several coats of hand-rubbed oil, I suddenly noticed that I had oriented one of the three legs so that the seam faced forward rather than to the side as with the other three legs. This was a minor mistake, but a mistake nonetheless.

Fortunately, at that time I remembered an old Shaker custom. In their tradition, only God can achieve perfection. Consequently, in each piece of furniture they consciously make a mistake and thereby avoid perfection. Clearly, without even trying, I was fulfilling this Shaker tradition. The skill that I was honing was the ability to chuckle at my foibles and move on.

Yet another skill that needs development is patience. This skill is necessary to keep yourself out of trouble. This need is best captured by the phrase "measure twice, cut once." One special class of frustration occurs when you suddenly realize that the pieces you just cut should have been cut longer. This violates a fundamental principle of woodworking.

With patience, you can minimize the frequency with which you run into such violations of immutable principles. You should persistently look for ways to save time by, for example, redesign or the use of jigs. However, once you have squeezed as much time as you can out of the manufacturing plan, you should calmly and patiently execute the plan. Take some time to smell the sawdust.

Assembly

Patience, and perhaps a few lessons learned and a chuckle or two, eventually leads to assembly. Everything literally comes together in assembly. Furniture emerges from a pile of pieces.

As noted earlier, it's a good idea to start with "dry" assembly. All pieces are assembled without glue or any fasteners. If joints are snug, and drawers, doors, and so forth, are accurate, it should be possible for this assembly to stand on its own, demonstrating your skill with your craft.

During the dry-assembly process, you can check for various aspects of fit and squareness. Will all the drawers open and close smoothly? Will the doors stay shut? There may be little problems, most of which can be easily corrected. Occasionally, a more sub-stantial correction is needed—for example, all the drawers are very slightly too wide. Such problems are much, much easier to solve if assembly has only been dry.

Glue is for keeps. Disassembly after gluing is more a matter of breaking apart than taking apart. In the process, many pieces are ruined. New pieces have to be cut. This often requires exten-sive setup, perhaps to cut a single piece.

In general, fixing problems downstream is time consuming, whether the product is a piece of furniture or, for example, an automobile. Problems due to inaccuracies are best resolved during prototyping, not final assembly. Problems due to design should be resolved even earlier. The least expensive way to solve problems is to anticipate them and redesign, recalibrate, and so on. Woodworking provides a domain where this principle is occasionally painfully demonstrated.

Once you are ready to glue, another principle—or perhaps a maxim—often emerges. You never have enough clamps. I was first told this by the man who sells me clamps. He's right. However, with a little ad hoc planning, I can usually arrange to glue in stages, with lunch, dinner, or a basketball game filling the time I wait for the glue to set before I can unclamp one assembly and clamp the next.

While this tactic works acceptably for hobbies, it does not work for real-life manufacturing. If the lack of clamps is a bottleneck that results in the inefficient use of personnel, you should consider acquiring more clamps or perhaps redesigning the product so that assembly does not require so many clamps. Inefficiencies like this can substantially increase the cost of a product without any increase in value or quality. Situations such as this should be identified and remediated during product planning and design rather than in manufacturing.

RELATIONSHIPS

Woodworking can be viewed as a fairly solitary activity. Much of it often is. However, relationships are central to woodworking. One set of relationships concerns users and customers.

As discussed earlier, many of your design choices are very much influenced by users' and customers' preferences in terms of aesthetics, functionality, durability, and price. In order to delight people, you need to interact with them sufficiently to understand their preferences and tradeoffs. Further, you may want their involvement and, hopefully, their enthusiasm along the way as the furniture emerges.

While relationships with users and customers are very important, other relations are more intimate. These relations involve your tools and the wood. It is essential that you understand the abilities and limitations of your tools, particularly as these abilities and limitations interact with your own. You need to understand and appreciate the human-machine system of which you are a part —not *the* central part, just an important part.

Similarly, you need to understand and appreciate the inclinations and preferences of the wood with which you are working. Wood will bend to your wishes to a certain extent. However, it will bend substantially if your wishes are aligned with its own. Then it will do wonderful things and truly delight you with its beauty, pliability, and strength.

We often tend to think of product design and manufacturing, if only implicitly, as a process of imposing our will on nature. We try to control tools and materials to achieve our ends. Similarly, as discussed in later chapters, we try to control organizations and other relationships with which we are involved. This often leads to conflict and frustration because tools, materials, organizations, and relationships will not bend. Sometimes they break in response to our impositions.

There is another model that we can adopt—collaboration. We can see ourselves, as well as the tools and wood, as part of an intentional system. We can study and learn our roles in this system, as well as the roles of our collaborators. From this perspective, the act of product design and planning is not a unilateral act of creation. It is a collaborative melding of inclinations and preferences. It is a process of mutual discovery.

I find myself amazed at what wood can become, at what tools can accomplish. Rather than a designer and creator, I feel like a facilitator. My role is to work with stakeholders, both animate and inanimate to coax creation out. Each lesson I learn, each time I laugh at myself, I try to remember that every experience can make me a better facilitator.

This process of collaboration and discovery can be filled with passion. There is the obvious joy of creation—assembling pieces to see furniture emerge. There are compelling noises and smells in the sawmill and in my shop—noises of tools, blades, gears, and belts; smells of wood, sawdust, glue, oils, and other finishes.

There are also shapes and patterns. Shapes of tools such as blades, fences, guides, and jigs. Shapes of milled edges. Shapes of mortises, tenons, and dovetails. The patterns of the wood are mystifying, made wonderful by oils rubbed again and again.

The passion for designing and planning products is, by no means, limited to furniture. My guess is that the innovativeness and quality of most products are linked to the passions of the stakeholders in these products. Passions of users and customers help to drive designers to pursue higher levels of creation. Passions of designers enable them to achieve these higher levels.

WOODWORKING AS A METAPHOR

It is easy to illustrate a wide range of product-planning concepts and principles in the context of woodworking. Furniture is a straightforward and very concrete product. Further, I am sure that my enthusiasm for woodworking is more than obvious.

Most people, however, plan other types of products. They design boats, clothing, computers, toys, and so on. As is illustrated in the next chapter, everything we have discussed in this chapter also applies in these other contexts. However, there are a variety of issues we have to consider in more depth in the process of generalizing the conclusions of this chapter.

A particularly important issue is the inscrutability of many markets. The furniture market is relatively straightforward—although I admittedly have greatly simplified it—compared to, for example, markets for new high-tech products where potential needs have to be inferred and demand created. Such products are considered in Chapter 3 using the planning, design, and development of software products as a case study.

This inscrutability of markets makes many questions more difficult to answer. What benefits do people expect from the products of interest? How many people want these benefits? How are purchases likely to be made? How much will people be willing to pay? It is much easier to answer questions like these for traditional products such as furniture than it is for less straightforward products.

For contexts where these types of questions are more difficult, a systematic product planning and design methodology can be important. In addition, methods and tools for both formulating and answering these questions are valuable. These types of support are considered at length in Chapter 3.

Another issue that often arises for new products is the maturity of the technology upon which such products are based. This issue is much less common for traditional products like furniture and, when it occurs, involves the process more often that the product. For some types of new products, the technology issues can be sufficiently substantial to raise questions about the technical feasibility of a product.

When dealing with new or rapidly evolving technologies, product planning and design have to explicitly address the risks associated with these technologies. For example, an evolutionary product family might be planned so that lower-risk technologies are employed in early versions of the products while, in parallel, R&D is pursued to lower the risks of the technologies that are to be employed in later versions of the products. An approach to managing risks in this way is discussed in Chapter 3.

Thus, product planning and design should not only consider and balance the issues discussed in this chapter in the context of woodworking. The planning process should also consider issues related to market intricacies, technology risks, and a variety of business-related issues that are discussed in later chapters. Fortunately, recognizing the plethora of issues and their relationships is the most difficult part. The methodologies elaborated in this book to help you deal with this range of issues are, for the most part, fairly simple and straightforward.

In light of my broadening of the set of planning issues in the closing pages of this chapter, it is perhaps useful to reconsider the utility of employing woodworking as our metaphor for product planning. It seems to me that woodworking provides somewhat narrow insights into the question of "What to build?" and very broad insights into the question of "How to build it?"

In Chapter 3, we take the "how" insights as givens and shift the balance of the discussion to addressing "what" in much more depth, particularly in relation to complex markets. In Chapters 4 and 5, attention shifts to "why" in terms of the business goals, strategies, and plans underlying pursuit of new products and markets.

3

Product
Planning

*Human-centered design is a process of assuring
that the concerns, values, and perceptions
of all stakeholders in a design effort
are considered and balanced.*

My strategy in this book is to begin explanations of each class of planning problem with concrete, easy-to-understand examples. The discussion then shifts to a broader and somewhat more abstract discussion of all aspects of the type of planning under consideration. This transition from specific and concrete illustrations to general and more abstract formulations is repeated three times in this book.

The rationale for this pattern is quite straightforward. Most people find it much easier to appreciate everyday types of illustrations. For example, from the discussions in Chapter 2, it should be clear why product-planning is needed for woodworking. The "grief" and "pain" that can result from not planning should be obvious. Thus, the stage is set.

However, it is likely that many readers are not yet quite sure of how to plan. Specifically, how can you create useful and usable product plans quickly? The goal of this chapter is to answer this question. The answer is presented in terms of a methodology that is illustrated in the contexts of a variety of examples.

It is essential that we begin this discussion by considering the nature of the problem of product-planning. In Chapter 2, we considered the questions of "What to build?" and "How to build it?"

My experience is that people and organizations are usually much better at answering the latter question. Given a description of what the marketplace requires, core competencies can be called upon to devise a means of satisfying these requirements.

In contrast, the question of "What to build?" often presents substantial difficulties. While most, if not all, people and enterprises would like to delight their constituencies, it tends to be difficult to determine what products, systems, and services are likely to be delightful. The answer to this question is often so elusive that people start working on the answer to the second question—how to build it—before they have reached closure on the first question.

As a result, many product plans are weak relative to "what," but strong on "how." The planning process becomes one of finishing the plan rather than creating a good plan. By good plan, I mean a series of steps that you can execute with reasonable confidence that the goals underlying the plan will be achieved.

The types of goals that should underlie product-planning are quite straightforward. The goal is to create and deliver a product, system, or service that will delight customers and thereby cause them to buy your offerings, support you with their votes, and so on. The only reasonable way to pursue this goal is to start by asking "What will delight our customers?"

This immediately begs the question "Who is the customer?" We tend to assume that the customer is the person who buys—who pays for—our products. This is, of course, true. However, sales are usually not this simple.

There are many situations in which the person who buys a product is different from the person who uses it. Thus, we can often distinguish customers from users. Customers typically focus on getting a good buy. Users, in contrast, are not as concerned with the purchase price. Instead, they focus on the usability and usefulness of the product.

Beyond customers and users, there are sometimes people who technically evaluate products. They usually do not buy or use the products they evaluate. Their job is to assess the extent to which a product is designed and built well. Further, they assess whether or not the product is designed appropriately for the purpose intended.

For some types of product-planning efforts, there are even more players in the game. For example, let's assume that your goal is to design and develop a new avionics—aviation electronics—product for use in commercial aircraft cockpits. Intuitively, you might think that you only have to convince the major aircraft companies, that is, Airbus, Boeing, or Douglas, to buy your product. Put simply, if you can delight one of these companies, you tend to think you will succeed.

However, these aircraft companies will not buy your product unless they have solid evidence that one of the major airlines wants it. Further, if they are interested, they will expect your product to be integrated with other avionics products and systems that they buy from avionics companies such as Bendix, Collins, Honeywell, Sextant, Smiths, and so forth. Thus, your sale now involves aircraft manufacturers, airlines, and avionics companies.

There are more players. The pilots union, and pilots in general, will be concerned with the usability and usefulness of your product. The machinists union, whose members maintain aircraft, are likely to be concerned with the maintainability of your product. The Federal Aviation Administration will require that your product be certified as flightworthy, which will require a very time-consuming and expensive process.

What at first may have seemed very simple—building a better avionics mousetrap—has become very complicated. There are many players in this game, with a wide range of interests. The product-planning problem concerns defining a product that will delight all of these players.

This example is representative of problems that involve many stakeholders—those who hold a stake in the outcomes of the product-planning and design process. As this example has illustrated, the concept of stakeholders is much broader than just users and customers. Stakeholders often include people who design, manufacture, service, and regulate the use of products and systems. Stakeholders can also include investors and lenders. As noted in earlier chapters, the concept of stakeholders plays a central role in this book.

HUMAN-CENTERED DESIGN

My approach to dealing with a multiplicity of stakeholders is called human-centered design. Human-centered design focuses on identifying stakeholders and assuring that their interests are understood. Products are then planned in a manner to assure that all stakeholders are delighted or, more realistically, the primary stakeholders are delighted and the secondary stakeholders are supportive.

I am sure that this approach sounds reasonable. The question, of course, is how to accomplish these ends. In particular, how can you systematically and efficiently keep track of all stakeholders, as well as their concerns, values, and perceptions?

A common way of dealing with complex problems is to develop a methodology that embodies appropriate principles and practices. Thus, a methodology for human-centered design is needed. Further, keeping in mind that users of this methodology are also stakeholders in the process of product-planning and design, it is important that this methodology, in itself, be usable and useful while also being simple.

After many experiences and attempts to develop a methodology for human-centered design, I came to realize that there are a core set of issues of concern to all stakeholders. The interpretation of each of these issues, as well as priorities among these issues, may vary considerably. Nevertheless, this set of issues is very straightforward and includes the issues listed in Figure 3.1. A central principle of human-centered design is that appropriate consideration and balancing of these four issues from the perspectives of all stakeholders will lead to a successful design.

Viability	Are the benefits of the solution sufficiently greater than its costs?
Acceptability	Do organizations/individuals adopt the solution?
Validity	Does the solution solve the problem?
Evaluation	Does the solution meet stated technical requirements?

Figure 3.1 Human-Centered Design Issues

There is an order in which these issues should be pursued. The natural order, at least for technology-oriented designers, is to start at the bottom and make sure that all technical issues are resolved first. For example, specific requirements such as size, weight, speed, and so on, are often the first issues pursued and resolved.

This bottom-up approach to product-planning and design often results in a technically excellent product that fails in the marketplace—for example, the $1 million depthfinder noted in Chapter 1. It is, at the very least, extremely inefficient to first get the technology right and then worry about the market. The difficulty, quite simply, is that this approach does not assure that the technology is right for the markets of eventual interest.

This technology-centered approach is inefficient in that it results in many technologies being developed but few technologies having eventual market value. You can adopt the Darwinian view that many technology mutations may be necessary in order for the fittest to prosper. My view, however, is that you can be much more creatively intentional and greatly increase your rate of success. You can do this by first focusing on the nature of market needs and desires.

This approach dictates that the list of human-centered design issues be addressed top down, starting with viability, moving on to acceptability, and so on. The technology-centered approach first asks questions such as, "Will it work?" In contrast, the human-centered approach begins with the question, "Who are the stakeholders and what matters to them?" At this point, the human-centered approach is not particularly concerned with what "it" is or will be.

Once stakeholders are identified, the next step is framing—determining the meaning of—viability, acceptability, and validity for each stakeholder or class of stakeholders. Framing viability involves determining what benefits each stakeholder seeks and how they conceptualize the costs of these benefits. This step also includes identifying measures whereby one can assess the extent of each type of benefit and cost.

People seek a wide variety of types of benefits. Food, clothing, and shelter are among our basic needs. However, we often desire many benefits beyond eating, feeling comfortable, and having a roof over our heads. For instance, we may want to perform tasks better or be enabled to perform tasks that we could not otherwise perform. We may want our work to be easier or quicker. Perhaps we seek aesthetic satisfaction or greater status.

The costs associated with benefits also may vary considerably. One class of stakeholder—customers—is usually concerned with the purchase price as a cost. For other classes of stakeholders, other types of costs are central. Users are concerned with the difficulties of learning to use, as well as using, a product or system. Maintainers are usually concerned with the difficulties of detecting, diagnosing, and repairing failures. Regulators will attach costs to, for example, compromises of safety. All stakeholders may perceive the fact of change as costly.

This discussion leads to the obvious question of whether or not benefits exceed costs. My experience, perhaps a consequence of getting older, is that most bright ideas do not produce benefits that exceed costs. For example, many types of technical analyses, although they are technically correct, are not worth the time and money required to perform them. Simple ballpark answers are often good enough and actually far superior in terms of benefits versus costs.

In the discussions of woodworking in Chapter 2, we noted that customers and users typically want furniture that is aesthetically pleasing, functional, durable, and inexpensive. Aesthetics is usually thought of as a benefit. Price is obviously one of the costs of obtaining this benefit. Thus, these two attributes are aspects of viability.

Functionality and durability are other types of issues. People usually do not buy a piece of furniture simply because it is durable. They may dismiss furniture that will not hold up or that is likely to need refinishing. They may not even consider furniture that is poorly constructed. These types of issues usually are not elements of cost-benefits tradeoffs.

One way to look at such issues is in terms of acceptability. Certain types of construction and finishes may not be acceptable. Similarly, particular types of woods and furniture styles may not be acceptable, perhaps because they are incompatible with other types of furniture already purchased.

Another class of issues surrounds validity. If I need a bureau, a chair is not a valid solution, even if it is aesthetically appealing, inexpensive, and durable. For a piece of furniture to be a valid alternative, it must provide the functionality desired.

Classification of issues seems straightforward—viability includes aesthetics and price, acceptability relates to durability, and validity concerns functionality. However, even for relatively simple products like furniture, there can be a few subtleties. For example, we may need to separate functionality into baseline functionality—for example, the essence of being a bureau—and additional functionality. Validity relates to the presence of baseline functionality. The potential benefits of additional functionality can be accounted for as elements of viability.

Thus, to be successful, a piece of furniture must clearly meet a need, satisfy this need in an acceptable way, and provide benefits that exceed costs. To assure success, therefore, you must determine what benefits are sought and how costs are conceptualized. You also must determine what influences acceptability—for example, barriers and avenues for change. Finally, you must determine how stakeholders will judge that a solution solves their problem.

Once you are confident of your answers to these questions, you are in a position to elaborate requirements. In other words, once you have framed viability, acceptability, and validity, and perhaps made some initial measurements using the measures associated with these three classes of issues, you should be able to define initial requirements for the product or system of interest.

Requirements are the characteristics that a product or system should have if it is to meet stakeholders' needs. For the evolving woodworking example, you would probably state requirements in terms of height, width, and depth of the bureau, as well as number of drawers, finish, and hardware. Perhaps that is all that is needed in your list of requirements.

It is easy to imagine, however, producing bureaus that would not succeed in the marketplace despite their satisfying these requirements. This might be due to your valid bureaus not being acceptable or viable. You might have the correct baseline functionality, but your bureaus might be unacceptable because you used plywood for interior pieces in a market that demands solid hardwoods throughout. Further, your competitors might provide additional functionality—for example, dust panels between drawers—that yields greater benefits with minimal increase in price.

You might respond to this illustration by saying that dust panels and hardwoods should have been stated in the requirements. Perhaps they should have been. However, the real problem is a failure of the product-planning process. Requirements should be such that resulting solutions will be not only valid, but also acceptable and viable. Thus, framing of these three issues should be done before requirements are defined.

This dictate poses a problem. My experience with a wide range of product-planning efforts is that there is tremendous pressure to get on with it and nail down requirements. There is often little patience with taking the time to truly understand stakeholders' needs and desires. Why is this so?

The reason is obvious. Designers in general are trained to get on with it. They are trained to employ their technical skills to solve problems. They gain much satisfaction, and often add much value, by applying these skills to creating things that provide benefits at reasonable costs.

However, my experience as an engineering professor—full time for over 10 years and part time for an additional 10 years—is that solving problems gets much more attention than formulating problems. In other words, creating a solution that meets requirements is allocated a far greater portion of the curriculum than is determining the requirements that will delight stakeholders and lead to market success. Put quite simply, we are not very good at teaching problem formulation.

A primary reason for this deficiency is a lack of methods for problem formulation. This lack has motivated much of my work in developing the product-planning methodology discussed in this chapter. This methodology focuses on framing, planning, refining, and completing measurements associated with the three central issues of viability, acceptability, and validity.

The methodology is pursued in the four phases listed in Figure 3.2. These phases are necessarily discussed in sequence, but are usually executed with much iteration and a degree of parallelism. Framing, planning, and measuring are pursued within each of these four phases using a variety of methods and tools ranging from questionnaires and interviews to mockups and prototypes.

Naturalist	Identifying, observing, and listening to stakeholders
Marketing	Obtaining stakeholders' reactions to alternative concepts
Engineering	Creating an evolutionary product family
Sales and Service	Obtaining reactions to products in use

Figure 3.2   Phases of Human-Centered Design

Naturalist Phase

The naturalist phase is a central construct within human-centered design. The term *naturalist* is drawn from anthropology and related disciplines. Two excellent examples of naturalists are Margaret Mead, who studied natives in Oceania, and Dian Fossey, who studied gorillas in Rwanda.

The primary activities in the naturalist phase are observing, listening, and interpreting. In the process, stakeholders are identified and the issues of viability, acceptability, and validity are framed. Put more simply, the naturalist phase serves to identify the players in the domain of interest and what is important to them.

The methods and tools employed in this process can include databases and directories to identify people and organizations, as well as to determine how many people and organizations of particular types exist. Questionnaires and structured interview techniques are often used to collect information relevant to viability, acceptability, and validity.

Most important in this process is the ability to observe and listen. When Margaret Mead and Dian Fossey performed their studies, they watched, took notes and pictures, and perhaps asked questions. They did *not* try to convince the natives or gorillas to change their ways of doing things or to buy anything. They were naturalizing, not marketing and selling.

While they were trained to observe and listen, most of us are not similarly trained. In fact, our typical education trains us to expound on our ideas, products, and services. We attempt to get others to understand and appreciate what we have to offer.

Observing and listening skills have to be consciously developed and refined. I use my frequent long aircraft flights to practice. I try to learn as much as I can about the business of the person sitting next to me. In this process, I do little talking. I ask simple questions, and the other person talks volumes.

I begin by introducing myself. I follow with straightforward questions such as:

- Are you headed home or out?
- What kind of business are you in?
- What are some of the difficult aspects of being in this business?
- What trends do you see affecting your business?

I typically work these questions in over two to three hours of talking. The rest of the time I just listen attentively and occasionally ask clarifying questions such as, "Why do you think that happens?"

My simple questions focus on this person's business and its central problems. When the person talks about alternative solutions, I ask questions that concern the viability, acceptability, and validity of solutions—although, I seldom use these terms. In this way, I have learned the intricacies of building bowling alleys, running a chain of laundries, selling electrical components, marketing medical devices, creating golf courses, and selling asphalt.

You might think that people would dread being next to me on an airplane! However, I have found that only about ten percent of my initiatives meet a deaf ear. Most people would prefer to have somebody to talk with, especially during meals. Further, and probably of more importance, my experience with hundreds of naturalist interviews is that people greatly value explaining their domains and problems to an attentive listener.

From my point of view, the process is fascinating. Patterns of issues and problems—mostly people-related problems—emerge repeatedly. Differences among domains are also apparent. For example, companies selling consumer electronics have very different concerns from those selling avionics systems for commercial aircraft.

The essence of the naturalist phase is the total focus on identifying and understanding stakeholders. As noted earlier, this emphasis is central to human-centered design. Unfortunately, very frequently this emphasis is missing. The reason for this is quite straightforward.

There is a natural tendency for us to assume that we know more than we do. For instance, if you have successfully been in the widget business for many years, you are likely to assume that you already understand the stakeholders in the widget domain. Further, you are likely to assume that you have solid understanding of related domains. Consequently, you may believe that you can sell derivatives of your widgets in these related domains with little if any additional focus on understanding stakeholders.

This tendency is, to an extent, a manifestation of the aforementioned impatience with problem formulation. We usually assume that we understand our problems and then focus on solutions. In fact, my experience is that our involvement with companies usually starts with their statement of a solution concept that they would like us to turn into a software product or system. Consequently, our first step often involves trying to infer the nature of the problem for which the stated solution is intended.

Fortunately, most of our customers are aware of our human-centered design workshops and tools. Consequently, they expect us to propose a four- to six-week period during which problem formulation is revisited and requirements are reviewed. This period often leads to important discoveries that profoundly affect the eventual solution.

For example, a major electronics manufacturer asked us to create a computer-based system and associated workstations for supporting the guards who are stationed at each entrance and exit of their plants. In a fairly short period, the design team was able to recast the problem in terms of access control rather than computer workstations. Further, the nature of the problem and the eventual solution were endorsed by all stakeholders because representatives of each group were involved in the process.

As another illustration, we were asked to design a graphical user interface for the passenger reservation system of a major airline. They hoped to overcome difficulties in learning to use, as well as in using, their existing system. The naturalist phase enabled identification of a wide range of stakeholders in this system, in particular, managers of products and services that were supposed to be sold via this system. The problem formulation that emerged emphasized the need for a sales-support system, staffed by sales-oriented personnel. The original emphasis on an easy-to-use flight database access system became only one of the objectives of a much broader effort.

Marketing Phase

The results of the naturalist phase include the identity of each class of stakeholder and the meaning of viability, acceptability, and validity for each of these classes. These results constitute a "theory" of the domain of interest. The purpose of the marketing phase is to test this theory, both directly and indirectly, in terms of alternative concepts for meeting needs in this domain.

This phase would perhaps better be called the marketing research phase because the focus is on gaining an understanding of how stakeholders are likely to react to alternative offerings. Thus, you are not marketing a specific product or service; rather, you are forming critical relationships with people who may become key customers once your offerings emerge.

The primary purpose of the marketing phase is to assess stakeholders' perceptions of alternative concepts in terms of viability, acceptability, and validity. Typically these assessments involve context-specific measures associated with these three issues. In other words, stakeholders are asked to characterize alternatives using the context-specific terminology, units of measure, and so forth, that they defined during the naturalist phase. It is the exception rather than the rule to ask stakeholders to respond directly in terms of viability, acceptability, and validity.

These assessments can be performed using a variety of methods and tools. Questionnaires and structured interviews are often used in conjunction with some representation of each concept. Typical forms of representation employed include sketches, scenarios, mockups, and prototypes. The objective is to employ the fastest and least expensive method that will yield the type of information needed.

To the extent possible, these assessments should employ multiple concepts, or at least wide variations on a single concept. The reason for this is to avoid self-fulfilling prophecies whereby a single concept is presented—usually your "pet" concept—and people respond positively primarily because they are not aware of alternatives. You then are convinced you have a winner, only to be undermined when your competition eventually shows people alternative concepts.

Unfortunately, lessons such as these are often learned very late in the product design and development process, perhaps when your product is already in the market. The methodology discussed in this chapter emphasizes dealing with these types of issues very early in the process. In this way, lessons are learned and bad news is dealt with long before it has become very expensive.

As noted earlier, the marketing phase is also used to test your evolving theory of the domain of interest. This can be done indirectly in terms of people's reactions to the utility of alternative concepts. Occasionally we make this assessment directly by, for example, asking people if scenarios embodying the concepts reasonably portray their jobs and tasks. In other words, we ask people to read stories that are intended to capture the nature of their jobs and to illustrate the ways in which concepts would affect their jobs. They are asked to assess the accuracy of the depiction of their jobs, as well as rate the concepts in terms of context-specific measures of viability, acceptability, and validity. In this way, you can learn, for instance, that a seeming problem with a particular concept results from a misperception about how a task is performed, not from the concept in itself.

The marketing phase can provide critical information. For example, we used written scenarios to portray a design information system for use by designers of aircraft cockpits. Designers assessed the concepts in these scenarios to be high in terms of viability and acceptability, but low to moderate for validity. Exploring this shortfall via follow-up interviews, people told us that we had portrayed designers accessing a variety of design databases that would be prohibitively expensive to create. We analytically studied this issue and determined that their perceptions were correct. This caused us to reassess the scope of this class of systems. Fortunately, this problem was identified and corrected very early in our efforts.

In another effort, we developed a software tool for analyzing tradeoffs between training personnel or using more sophisticated aiding technologies that would enable the use of less skilled personnel. Put simply, this tradeoff involves deciding how much "smarts" to put in people and how much "smarts" to put in machines. The purpose of this tool is to assist analysts and designers in determining what type of training is needed, as well as what additional system functionality is required, to satisfy performance requirements. This tool employs computational models to predict the impact of any particular combination of training and aiding.

During the naturalist phase, we identified, in the military and in industries such as automobiles and insurance, a variety of stakeholders in this tradeoff. We talked with many opinion leaders in these domains, and they confirmed the importance of this tradeoff. They indicated, however, that this tradeoff was seldom explicitly addressed because there were no tools available for resolving this issue.

This seemed to be a great opportunity—a problem that everyone agrees is important but for which there is, as yet, no solution. On the other hand, it posed a dilemma for our product planning. We could not study people currently dealing with this tradeoff and frame viability, acceptability, and validity in the usual way. Our solution was to ask a set of opinion leaders to serve as surrogate users.

We developed a shallow prototype that illustrated how such a tool might work, although below the human-computer interface the actual functionality did not exist. Our surrogate users spent an afternoon reviewing this prototype in terms of viability, acceptability, and validity. More specifically, we asked them if the training-versus-aiding problem could be successfully addressed using this tool (validity), whether the approach was usable by typical analysts and designers (acceptability), and if the benefits of using the tool would exceed the cost of becoming proficient in its use (viability). They concluded that our concept was potentially viable but had acceptability and validity problems.

The source of these problems was our assumption about the range of likely users of this tool. We had implicitly assumed that all users would have the same background and skills as we do—namely, intimate knowledge of training and aiding alternatives, as well as skills with formulating and using computational models. Once the surrogate users pointed out that we had, in effect, made such assumptions, and that they were incorrect, it was clear that substantial changes were needed.

We very carefully reconsidered the nature of the tool for novice, journeyman, and expert users. Abilities and limitations of each class of user were hypothesized. These analyses led to greatly expanded functionality within a new prototype of the tradeoff analysis tool. A review by our surrogate users led to the conclusion that we were closer but not yet there. Additional analyses and a third prototype led them to conclude that we had hit the target.

This vignette serves to illustrate how the marketing phase is used to test and revise hypotheses regarding the nature of stakeholders in terms of their abilities, limitations, and preferences. In the naturalist phase, we had correctly identified an important problem. However, we had not identified the abilities and limitations of the likely problem solvers. The prototyping process, as well as the panel of surrogate users, enabled us to identify our incorrect *implicit* assumptions and to correct these assumptions.

The results of the marketing phase include a tested and usually revised theory of the domain of interest. In addition, one or more concepts will have been assessed in terms of viability, acceptability, and validity. This assessment typically leads to one of these concepts being chosen as superior in the sense that it is the most likely to delight stakeholders. In the process of making this choice, the chosen concept is often modified substantially due to one or more stakeholders' perceptions of viability, acceptability, or validity problems.

Engineering Phase

The results of both the naturalist and marketing phases form the basis for the engineering phase. The purpose of the engineering phase is to transform conceptual functionality into physical reality. This includes design, development, manufacturing, packaging, and delivery of the product or system. These activities include consideration of many of the issues that emerged in the discussion of woodworking, that is, designing for manufacturability, materials planning, use of tools and jigs, roles of prototypes, and assembly.

This phase begins with the drafting of an Objectives Document that reflects the results of the naturalist and marketing phases. This document succinctly summarizes the "why" of the product-planning and design effort. This information provides an important foundation for later preparation of requirements documentation. This foundation is of greatest value when requirements evolve and change, leading to many design iterations.

The Objectives Document includes three elements: goals, functions, and objectives. Goals are often broad and sometimes philosophical. Goals often include overall statements of benefits sought, such as substantial improvement in productivity or reduction of paperwork. Goals also tend to include things such as improved access for the handicapped and greater opportunities for job enrichment.

The Objectives Document also outlines the conceptual functionality necessary for achieving goals. For example, the goal of reducing paperwork might lead to specification of functions for creating, editing, storing, and retrieving the information previously captured on paper. For each function, one or more objectives are listed that specify what must be accomplished to enable this function. The retrieval function, for example, might include objectives for identifying, locating, accessing, and displaying information.

Note that the Objectives Document does not specify *how* these functions and objectives are to be realized. This document describes only *what* the product or system is to include. Subsequent documents for requirements, conceptual design, and detailed design are progressively concerned with how the product or system functions.

My experience is that documents for requirements, conceptual design, and detailed design are pretty much standard fare in many product-planning and design efforts—so much so that I need not detail such documentation in this chapter. However, Objectives Documents or the equivalent are seldom prepared. Consequently, as design and development proceed, it is quite common for people to forget why certain requirements exist. Further, they often face tradeoffs where two or more alternatives appear to be equivalent. Without broader philosophical guidance, arbitrary choices are often made. Information on goals, for instance, can enable better choices.

When there are many stakeholders and a large number of measures associated with the issues of viability, acceptability, and validity, it can be difficult to reach consensus on one set of goals, functions, and objectives. It can be much more difficult to agree on a set of requirements and a single conceptual design. I have found that these difficulties can be substantially reduced by employing the concept of evolutionary design and, in particular, the construct of evolutionary architectures.

The basic idea of evolutionary design is that the ultimate product or system cannot be designed without iteration and evolution—basically, you cannot get it completely right the first time. Given this premise, evolutionary design involves planning a series of products, or a product family, that evolves toward becoming the ultimate.

The concept of evolutionary design is embodied in the construct of evolutionary architectures. Use of this construct involves planning three levels of a product. These levels are termed A, B, and C, definitions of which are shown in Figure 3.3.

Level A	The Baseline: What you know you can do.
Level B	Bridging Concept: What you are willing to promise.
Level C	The Vision: What you would like to do.

Figure 3.3   Evolutionary Architectures

Use of this construct begins with Level C—the vision of the ultimate product or system. Definition of the vision is based on understanding stakeholders' concerns, values, and perceptions, expressed in terms of context-specific measures of viability, acceptability, and validity. The vision is the product or system that would delight all stakeholders, or at least the primary stakeholders.

The vision embodied by Level C is defined independent of time, money, resources, and technological feasibility. The question at this point is *not* whether the vision can be realized. Your sole concern should be with delighting the marketplace. In other words, "Can we do it?" is not asked. "Do they want it?" is the reigning question.

Once Level C is defined, attention is shifted to Level A—the baseline. This level defines the product that will be sold first, perhaps this year or soon thereafter. Level A is how you put bread and butter on the table. Consequently, the baseline inevitably relies on existing competencies and resources.

Level A is defined relative to Level C in terms of a subset of the ultimate product functionality, or perhaps in terms of reduced performance (e.g., slower, less efficient) relative to Level C. In this way, the "futurity" of Level A—not the futility—is assured. This is one of the most important reasons for defining Level C before Level A. If the baseline is defined first, I have found that it becomes an anchor on your thoughts, always dragging your perspective back to today's reality rather than tomorrow's potentiality.

Once Level C and then Level A are defined, the emphasis shifts to Level B—the bridging concept. Level B represents the next substantial evolutionary step from Level A toward Level C. The bridging concept provides stakeholders with significantly greater benefits than the baseline.

While it might seem that Level C is the next step from Level B, this is not the way it usually works. Level C is never achieved! This is due to expansion of the vision as elements of Level B become integrated into the new Level A. Thus, you are always selling Level A, researching and developing Level B, and conceptualizing Level C. As elements of Level B are achieved, they are shifted to Level A. These achievements cause the notion of Level C to be expanded, which sets the new agenda for Level B.

There are two important principles associated with the construct of evolutionary architectures. The first principle is concerned with assuring that a natural evolutionary product family is created:

First Principle: The underlying conceptual architecture should be capable of supporting Levels A, B, and C.

This principle dictates that the functionality of Level A be a subset of Level B, and the functionality of Level B be a subset of Level C. Further, to satisfy this principle, there must be a clear and useful evolutionary path that will motivate stakeholders to upgrade from one level to another as new generations of the product or system emerge.

The second principle concerns the desired relationship between the evolving product family and the stakeholders in this product. This principle focuses on creating continuing demand for the product family's evolution:

Second Principle: *Intrigue* stakeholders with Level C, *market* them Level B, and *sell* them Level A.

The best way to intrigue stakeholders is to assure them that you and they have a shared vision of what will ultimately delight them. Similarly, the best way to market new capabilities is to have stakeholders involved with defining these capabilities. Finally, it is essential that there be shared expectations of what will actually be delivered next.

The evolutionary architectures construct and associated principles are very powerful. My experience is that the enterprises with whom I work adopt this construct almost immediately. Put very simply, it works!

A frequent question is "How do I avoid the situation where customers are paying for Level A, but expecting Level C?" The answer is quite straightforward—tell them all about the notions of Levels A, B, and C. You should solicit their inputs and, better yet, their active participation in defining the vision (Level C) and the bridging concept (Level B). You should collaborate with them to create an evolutionary product family that will delight them.

Another question that frequently arises concerns partitioning capabilities among Levels A, B, and C. I use a few simple rules to make these decisions. First of all, as noted earlier, Level C should be totally stakeholder driven, with little regard for the problems of actually realizing this vision. About the only things that I exclude are teleportation and perpetual motion.

In contrast, Level A should be totally concrete. There should be no remaining R&D issues. Manufacturing requirements should be completely clear and readily satisfiable. Needs for services and product support should be completely defined.

Level B bridges from Level A toward Level C. As such there should be some open issues associated with R&D, manufacturing, and service. Typically, these issues are such that they are likely to be resolved in a time frame that will enable a new product generation that is competitive relative to what is expected in the industry of interest—perhaps one to two years in software and two to five years in hardware, for example.

The woodworking issues discussed in Chapter 2 also affect the partitioning of capabilities among Levels A, B, and C. Since Level A should be delivered to the marketplace in a timely fashion, this baseline product has to be manufacturable in this time frame. This may mean that Level A has to be much simpler—less functionality or performance—than may be technically possible. This may be necessary because available manufacturing processes cannot reliably produce the quantity and quality desired within the time constraints adopted.

In Chapter 2, I noted that producing 12 wooden stools within tight time constraints required simplifying the design to make the stools more easily manufactured. Similarly, as illustrated later in this chapter, our initial releases of software products are often simplified in order to get them into the market faster, with subsequent releases adding substantial functionality.

Thus, the choice of functionality to be included in Level A depends not only on design and development of the product itself. This choice is also highly affected by how long it will take to manufacture, package, and deliver the product or system. This time includes whatever time is necessary to design and develop the manufacturing, packaging, and means of delivery or distribution.

To the extent that these capabilities are available "off the shelf," Level A can make it to the market faster and include more functionality.

The partitioning of functionality, as well as of performance requirements for these functions, depends on understanding the market's needs and desires and the ways in which these needs and desires can be satisfied. The issues discussed in Chapter 2, that is, designing for manufacturability, materials planning, use of tools and jigs, roles of protoypes, and assembly, are all central to deciding what can be delivered first (Level A), what will have to wait for the next major upgrade (Level B), and what must remain in the realm of R&D (Level C).

The partitioning process should, at the very least, involve people concerned with marketing and sales (i.e., what customers want); design (i.e., how to provide it); manufacturing (i.e., how to fabricate it); and finance (i.e., what it will cost). All of these issues should be considered early and in parallel. Concurrent engineering is a phrase used to denote this type of product-planning and design process. Put simply, concurrent engineering is a way in which all the issues in Chapters 2 and 3 can be considered simultaneously in the product-planning process.

To a great extent, the tradeoffs associated with evolutionary design can be fully resolved only by also considering a variety of business issues. These issues are considered in Chapter 5. The discussions in that chapter draw substantially on the concept of evolutionary design, the construct of evolutionary architectures, and the distinctions between Levels A, B, and C.

Sales and Service Phase

The fourth and final phase of the product-planning methodology—the sales and service phase—is not directly concerned with selling and servicing products or systems. Instead, given that the product or system has been sold and is being serviced, this phase focuses on creating and maintaining relationships.

The purpose of this phase is to follow the product or system into use and gain closure on viability, acceptability, and validity. In this process, one goal is to assure that expectations have been met. An equally important goal is to assess and understand the nature of rising expectations that should influence which elements of Level B next migrate to Level A.

This phase also involves building relationships with key stakeholders who can become the advocates or champions of your product or system within their organization and perhaps more broadly. These people can help you to refine and revise measures of viability, acceptability, and validity, as well as aspiration levels for these measures. In this way, the sales and service phase can accelerate the next naturalist and marketing phases. Thus, there is continual iteration, in addition to much more parallelism than I have portrayed here, among phases of the product-planning process as the product family evolves.

CASE STUDY

The remainder of this chapter is devoted to a case study. Thus far, a variety of vignettes has been utilized to illustrate the elements of the product-planning and design methodology. This provides the basis for presenting a case study in its entirety. This case study focuses on the conceptualization, design, development, marketing, and sales of software tools that support planning.

I hasten to note that this case study involves software tools created and sold by my company. I chose this case study because of my intimate knowledge of its evolution. To the extent possible, I have tried to emphasize the process whereby these tools emerged, rather than the specific nature of these products. My goal is to provide you with a compelling example of human-centered design rather than convince you of the merits of these particular tools.

It is useful to start by considering how the idea for this product family arose. Traditionally, our business has been focused on engineering services and contract R&D in the aerospace, electronics, and computer industries. We typically develop proof-of-concept products or systems, for example, a training simulator, which are delivered to our customers along with data from studies using these concept simulators.

Our competitive advantage in these efforts is our concepts, principles, methods, and tools for dealing with human-related issues in complex systems. In addition, we have proprietary technology for creating "intelligent interfaces." This technology involves embedding in the interface software explicit representations of users and their goals, plans, and tasks. These representations enable systems to anticipate users' needs and tailor the support provided to these needs. Typical applications involve software for training or directly supporting (i.e., aiding) operators and maintainers of complex systems.

Roughly five years ago, several of our customers asked us to teach them how we conceptualize such applications. In response to this request, we developed a five-day seminar on human-centered design. This seminar focused on an earlier version of the material discussed in this chapter. After we had presented this seminar several times, we were asked to create a one-day version of this seminar for top management. We happily responded since we were primarily serving our mainstream customers.

These presentations to top management led to a new request. Could we apply human-centered design to improving organizational processes in general, and strategic business planning in particular? This request led, after many iterations, to the methodology discussed in Chapter 5.

As these two methodologies matured via repeated applications, we began to envision how the use of these methodologies could be supported by software tools. In addition, discussions with customers frequently resulted in their requests that we accelerate the development of such tools.

Naturalist Phase

At this point, we started the naturalist phase. Obviously, we did not start with a "clean slate." However, this was the point at which we started to seriously consider the stakeholders, as well as the issues of viability, acceptability, and validity, in planning. In particular, we initially focused on the typical stakeholders in planning processes and their perceptions of the benefits and costs associated with improving these processes.

We began by focusing on our customers—Fortune 500, technology-based companies and government agencies with technology-oriented programs. The primary stakeholders in planning were found to include those charged with developing product or program plans, managers of planning functions that coordinate all planning, and managers of finance functions that are responsible for combining and analyzing the financial implications of all the enterprise's plans. Interestingly, we rarely found top management—the executive office—involved in strategic business planning in other than a very broad sense.

In these companies and agencies, we found that the people charged with planning were often people with technical backgrounds who had risen through the ranks and now had major responsibilities. For these types of people, new-product planning and strategic business planning were not natural acts. They often struggled with these tasks and encountered the types of difficulties discussed in Chapter 1.

In contrast, those in charge of planning and finance functions knew more about planning, but could not prepare other people's plans for them. If they attempted this, the resulting plans would inevitably be viewed as "their" plans, and there would be great risk that the people who had to execute the plans would not buy in and feel ownership.

Thus, the typical situation was that the people who had to create plans had neither the training nor orientation to do so, and those with the training and orientation necessarily were limited to serving as coordinators. Since the people who had to plan did not highly value the activity, the primary benefit sought from a method or tool was the ability to develop good plans quickly. The time required to develop good plans was viewed as the predominant cost.

This conclusion begs the question "What is a good plan?" Intuitively, one might say that a good plan leads to good consequences, for example, sales and profits. However, I think that this is much too strict a test. Further, these measures prohibit you from knowing if your plan is good until after it has been imple-mented and run its course.

I hold that a good plan can be judged plan is good if the team associated with it with confidence. A plan is good if the team strategies, and course of action make sense to the desired consequences.

This definition of goodness provides ample opportunity for teams to delude themselves, perhaps because they want to get on with it. This tendency can be overcome, or at least minimized, by using cross-functional planning teams. For instance, teams might include people from marketing, engineering, manufacturing, finance, and product support.

With an initial grasp of viability, we proceeded to consider acceptability and validity. For the types of technology-oriented enterprises that are our customers, there were, and still are, few acceptability issues related to inhibitions about using computers. However, there was concern that our solution be compatible with their computing infrastructure.

On this issue, we happened to be at the right place at the right time. Most, if not all, of these enterprises were in the process of weaning themselves from mainframe computers and, in some cases, from high-end workstations. To be acceptable, our software tools would have to fit into distributed, desktop-computing environments. Further, while this still left us three choices, the overwhelming majority of our customers wanted our software to run on a personal computer using Microsoft Windows™.

I would like to be able to claim that we anticipated the dramatic shift in computing paradigms from mainframe computers to distributed, desktop microcomputers. However, to be very honest, it was serendipity. Fortunately, due to our approach to product-planning, by listening very carefully to our customers, we had placed ourselves in the path of serendipity.

The implication is that we believe our stakeholders to be smarter than we are relative to their problems and the trends that are affecting their enterprises. We know how to create certain types of solutions. However, we must observe and listen carefully to understand the stakeholders' context. The naturalist phase and, to an extent, the marketing phase are the mechanisms whereby this observing and listening are orchestrated.

Two sets of issues involved both acceptability and validity. ᵔe of these was the functionality provided by our tools. Beyond ᵔrting use of the methodologies discussed in Chapters 3, 5, ᵔ our tools also require word processing, spreadsheet, and ᵔanagement capabilities. We initially thought that customers would use readily available, off-the-shelf software for these capabilities. When we asked customers if this was a good assumption, we found that 100 percent of our customers did *not* want to have to access multiple tools. They wanted our planning tools to be self-contained in the sense that they would not be required to access other tools in order to proceed.

On the other hand, they also wanted to be able to access other tools if they chose to do so. Further, they wanted to be able to move seamlessly among our multiple tools. While the Windows environment helps to deal with this issue, the level of seamlessness that customers want far exceeds what is currently available.

The implication of this desire is that we have had to include much more functionality in our Level A tools than originally imagined. At the same time, our vision for Level C, and for Level B to the extent possible, reflects the seamlessness that customers want, but we do not yet know the best way to provide. The Levels A, B, and C for these tools are discussed at length later in this chapter.

Another functionality issue concerned the extent of the financial projections provided by the software. The philosophy underlying our concepts and methods emphasizes stakeholders and market needs rather than numbers. To a great extent, the appeal of our approach has been the discarding of strict planning by the numbers. As a consequence, we tended to downplay the financial projections within the planning process.

However, we quickly discovered that the finance function within enterprises is a very key stakeholder in planning. With this discovery came a surprise. Many people in finance were ardent advocates of our approach. At the same time, they said, "While being market driven is essential and numbers are not all that counts, you nevertheless have to get the numbers right."

This orientation led several customers to help us to add necessary functionality in the financial area without making that functionality dominant. Speadsheet capabilities were expanded and the ability to project year-end financial statements, across all plans, for each year of the overall plan was added. With these additions, people within the finance function of enterprises have become among our strongest advocates.

The second set of issues that involves both acceptability and validity relates to implementation concerns. When we queried customers with regard to pricing our software—a viability issue—they said that our anticipated prices were fine, perhaps even unnecessarily low. They added, however, that they were less concerned with the cost of acquiring our tools than with the cost of being successful with our tools.

As we pursued this issue further, we often found that they were quite uncertain about their abilities to adopt and utilize what they perceived as being a very appealing approach to planning. Put simply, they questioned the acceptability of buying our software off the shelf, as well as the validity of a solution that did not include assistance with implementation problems.

We handled these concerns in two ways. First, we modified our workshop offerings to include training and coaching in use of the software tools for those customers who purchased the software in conjunction with a workshop. Second, we bundled follow-up consulting services with our proposals to customers. This, obviously, increased the price, but customers feel that such proposals are more realistic.

From the above discussion, it should be very clear that our customers have had very substantial impacts on the tools we have created. By framing their concerns in terms of viability, acceptability, and validity issues, we were able to interpret the basis for these concerns. This enabled us to know how to modify the tools as well as how to package these offerings.

How was all of this information gathered? As noted earlier, my frequent seminars and workshops provided the initial impetus for planning the development of the software tools. Once we became serious, we formalized the naturalist phase using a variety of interviews to gain better understanding of stakeholders and to frame viability, acceptability, and validity. These interviews were usually conducted in conjunction with being at a customer's facility for a workshop and/or a sales call.

Marketing Phase

The marketing phase involved obtaining customers' reactions to a series of prototypes. For a brief period of time, the prototype involved only a paper portrayal of each planning methodology in terms of flowcharts, tables, and assessment hierarchies. Fairly soon, we transitioned to a computer-based prototype developed using a rapid prototyping language.

This prototype provided many insights. Customers were very much impressed with what we were trying to develop. However, over 90 percent of those who viewed this prototype said that we would have to use different computer hardware than was used for this prototype. Namely, our software tools would have to run on personal computers with Microsoft Windows, if we expected them to buy these tools. We took these responses very seriously.

The next prototype was what is called a beta version of software. It was fully functional and now ran on the customers' preferred computer with the preferred operating environment. Several customers reviewed this version. A few customers bought this version, with the agreement that they would get subsequent versions for no additional cost.

Use of this prototype and a subsequent version led to many of the insights noted earlier regarding functionality in general, and the financial aspects of one of the tools in particular. Two of the tools are now on the market, with new versions planned for release every six to twelve months. One of these tools was substantially modified after beta assessments and again released to the market for additional beta assessments prior to format release. A third tool is, as of this writing, being evaluated in prototype form.

This process sounds much smoother than it actually was. Perhaps the biggest problem we encountered was the planning tool that was just noted as being substantially modified after beta assessments. The design and development of the first beta version of this tool was based on the functionality customers told us they wanted. We included everything they asked for.

The result was a tool that was overwhelming. There were too many options and too many paths. It was difficult for users to keep track of relationships among all the pieces of information being generated. Based on these reactions, this tool was substantially redesigned and, as you might expect, the schedule slipped significantly. Several customers who were anxious to have the functionality this tool provides had to wait far too long.

This is a good example of trying to be very responsive to the market but not thinking through the implications of giving customers everything they requested. Of course, customers had not thought it through either, and that is why they were patient with us. Nevertheless, it was our problem, not theirs.

Thus, good human-centered design is not simply a matter of providing customers with exactly what they request. It is also important to understand the basis of their requests, in terms of viability, acceptability, and validity. Beyond the basis of their requests, you need to understand the implications of fulfilling them. If the implications are undesirable, then understanding the basis can be used to help customers reformulate their needs.

Engineering Phase

The information compiled during the naturalist and marketing phases led to initial definition of an evolutionary product family at the beginning of the engineering phase. This initial definition has been refined and revised as these software tools have been used by more and more customers. In this way, the market for these tools drives the evolving vision of this product family.

The vision—Level C—includes a set of software tools for new-product planning and design, strategic planning and management, and planning and implementing organizational change. These tools have common user interfaces and underlying data structures, the combination of which enables users to move seamlessly among these tools. Setup tools enable users to configure these tools and tailor them to their own organizations. Enterprise-specific terminology, policies, procedures, and knowledge bases can be integrated into these tools. Tools provided by other vendors can also be linked seamlessly to our tools.

The planning, design, and management environment these offerings provide can be used in both aiding and training modes. The aiding mode provides data, procedures, guidance, expert advice, and group support that directly augments performance of the tasks associated with planning.

These types of support make it very clear what is to be done, assure that it is accomplished efficiently, and greatly increase the opportunities to produce good plans.

The other mode within this environment is training. On-line tutorials and simulations provide the means for just-in-time learning. Computer-based agents provide coaching and advice in general. Animation, multi-media, and other technologies enable creation of a virtual organizational reality, within which users can experience the marketplace, factories, and offices with a variety of organizational scenarios, either from the library or designed by them. Using the capabilities provided by this learning environment, users can dramatically improve their potential to perform, while also designing their future environments.

With these types of tools and technologies on everybody's desk, table, or lap, activities associated with planning, design, and management are performed in a very distributed manner. People in the executive suite, shop floor, and customers' marketing and sales departments, as well as key people on vacation, can all interact to envision alternative futures, formulate plans, diagnose planning and execution problems, and assess results.

The frequency with which people are in face-to-face contact and work together is greatly increased by these tools and technologies. However, due to the power and affordability of these and other computer and communications technologies, people travel on business much less. The huge savings in travel costs and the dramatic increases in productivity due to people not spending much of their time in cars, airports, and airplanes produce profits that dwarf the costs of these technologies.

When business travel is necessary, people have the same planning, design, and management environments in their aircraft seats. In fact, the airlines that provide the best of these environments are the most profitable. The airplane itself, at least from the point of view of the business passenger, has become a computer cabinet and is taken for granted. The value added has become the information environment and associated utilities provided.

My experience is that most of our customers find this vision very compelling—they are intrigued. They also know that neither we nor our competitors can provide these capabilities. We readily tell them this. For Level C, the only concern is that they want it, not that we can do it—yet!

What we can give them is Level A, the baseline. We can also engage them in creating Level B, the bridging concept. Thus, as prescribed by the principles of evolutionary design discussed earlier, we try to intrigue customers with Level C, market them Level B, and sell them Level A.

Level A—the baseline—is how we secure sales, cash flow, and profits. This dictates that we get baseline products into the market quickly. Two issues affect how quickly we can succeed. One issue concerns our abilities to design, develop, and test products, which affects when products are ready. The second issue is related to customers' abilities to adopt and utilize products, which strongly influences how long it takes to make sales.

The time associated with both of these issues can be decreased by keeping Level A offerings as simple as possible while also providing enough value added to justify the price you must charge to cover your costs and return a profit. The business issues associated with these software tools are discussed in Chapter 5. It is nevertheless useful to note in this chapter the strong influence that such issues have on defining Level A offerings versus their subsequent Level B upgrades.

This line of reasoning led us to define our Level A software tools as three independent packages for new product-planning, strategic business planning, and analysis of organizational changes stemming from product and business plans. While these tools have a common conceptual basis and all reflect a human-centered design philosophy, they do not play together seamlessly. Further, capabilities for tracking plans as they are implemented are quite limited.

These limitations are primary targets for Level B upgrades. Also targeted are performance improvements in terms of decreased memory requirements, faster file access times, and improved speed in general. In addition, there is a long list of very specific features and improvements that one or more customers have requested.

Level B also involves a few issues that are being addressed by R&D efforts. One issue concerns evolving the indirect support that Level A provides for group collaboration to functionality that directly supports collaborative work. Another issue concerns use of animation, multimedia, and related technologies for enhanced on-line tutoring and coaching. These types of issues are also being pursued as they relate to the long-term Level C vision rather than just the Level B bridging concept that needs to reach the market in the next two to three years.

A central tension exits between allowing technologies to mature as Level B efforts versus rushing to get as much as possible of Level B into the next Level A to gain a market advantage. If you push too fast, customers may end up with shaky technology that undermines their confidence in your product and you. On the other hand, if you are too cautious, your product, and perhaps you, may be viewed as out of date.

The evolutionary architectures construct can help in this regard. It is not necessary to have crisp distinctions between Levels A and B. You can treat these two levels as ends of a continuum of functionality and provide a steady stream of product upgrades. This tends, however, to require that careful attention be paid to manufacturability issues such as discussed in Chapter 2. In particular, transitioning functionality from proof-of-concept prototypes to well-engineered software products is a process that should be carefully managed to avoid problems associated with poor-quality code creeping into supposedly finished products.

Having repeatedly addressed the issues associated with partitioning functionality among Levels A, B, and C, we have been able to slowly improve our abilities to implement concurrent engineering. Manufacturability has become a key element of software design decisions. Software analogs of tools and jigs are a priority. Extensive prototyping enables creation of very early versions of tools that we enlist our key customers to evaluate, as you might expect, in terms of viability, acceptability, and validity. Thus, while software development and woodworking are by no means identical, the metaphorical linkages are quite clear.

Sales and Service Phase

The ongoing sales and service phase for these software tools is an important element of the product-planning process. In the first 18 months that these tools were in the market, roughly 1,000 copies were sold to about 20 large enterprises. A typical sale was a site license of 25 copies for use within a single enterprise.

Perhaps 50 percent of these enterprises systematically expanded the use of these tools throughout their organization. We paid, and continue to pay, careful attention to these enterprises. First of all, we want to make sure that they are satisfied with these tools.

Just as important, we want to understand how they are using the tools. Our experience has been that customers are often very creative in the ways they use our tools. We want to know about these new applications. Sometimes they hit the limits of what the current versions of these tools can do. This information is also useful to help us understand what new functionality is needed.

In general, active users are the best source of ideas for product upgrades. By systematically paying attention to what they suggest, we have a much greater chance of delighting them with new versions. Also, we greatly decrease the likelihood that they will defect to other tools.

This ongoing process, which is the essence of the sales and service phase, is best characterized as collaborative product-planning and design. This collaboration can greatly expedite subsequent naturalist and marketing phases. To a great extent, our company has evolved into a role of facilitating our customers' design of the types of tools they will inherently find delightful.

This type of relationship with customers is very different than traditional arm's-length relationships. As such, it can threaten many long-held, and often implicit, beliefs about customers' needs and desires, roles of technology and innovation, and related issues. These beliefs can tend to get in the way of successful human-centered design. An approach to understanding the nature and roles of such beliefs is discussed in Chapter 7.

SUMMARY

This chapter has introduced and elaborated a variety of concepts that are central to many of the discussions in subsequent chapters. One of these concepts is stakeholders. Identifying and understanding stakeholders are essential for successful product-planning and design.

Another important concept is the core issues of viability, acceptability, and validity. These issues should be framed—defined in terms of benefits, costs, and so forth—prior to formalizing requirements. This will help you to assure that products and systems solve the right problem, solve it in an agreeable way, and provide benefits that exceed the costs of the solution.

The framing, planning, and measuring associated with these issues can be pursued efficiently in terms of the four phases of human-centered design—naturalist, marketing, engineering, and sales and service. Using methods and tools such as questionnaires, interviews, scenarios, mockups, and prototypes, the activities of these phases can lead to timely answers to central product-planning and design questions.

The information compiled in this way can be captured succinctly in an Objectives Document that describes the goals, functions, and objectives of the product-planning, design, and development effort. This document provides an important basis for subsequent design documentation. It also provides an audit trail from the designed product back to the analyses and studies that provided the initial design rationale and concepts. These types of linkages can be invaluable when your products have to be modified or redesigned.

The concepts just summarized provide a basis for evolutionary design of product families that will delight stakeholders and commit them to the successive versions of products on the evolutionary path from Level A to Level B and toward Level C. If the human-centered design methodology is followed, stakeholders will be intrigued with Level C, especially if they have participated in defining this vision. Their mid-term expectations will be that the next major upgrade of capabilities is captured by the definition of

Level B. Finally, they will be awaiting—or have just received—Level A, which will meet their near-term expectations.

Stakeholders in general, and customers in particular, participate in the definition and evolution of levels A, B, and C as collaborators. In the past, they may have had to pin down their needs in terms of requirements, which they then passed, often with some trepidation, over to engineering staffs or outside contractors. Now they are full participants and can learn from the product-planning, design, and development process. They can, in this way, come to understand their own needs and preferences. They can also assure that they are delighted with the products of the collaborative effort.

4

Hiking

Hiking is a process whereby you and the trail uncover and create where each other is going.

I discussed product planning in Chapters 2 and 3. The emphasis was on devising goals, strategies, and plans that enable creation of artifacts or things. While I acknowledged the fact that these things would have to be designed, developed, manufactured, marketed, sold, and serviced, I did not pay any attention to the nature of the organization or organizations necessary to make this happen. Temporarily, at least, you did not have to concern yourself with the enterprise that would have to be created—or perhaps re-created—in order to succeed in the marketplace with, for example, your furniture or software tools.

In this chapter and the next, the issues associated with creating such enterprises are addressed. The topic is business planning, in a broad sense that includes large and small companies, public institutions, government agencies, and so on. Thus, rather than planning and designing a product, in these chapters we focus on planning and designing enterprises.

Business planning often tends to be complicated and confusing. Many issues and tradeoffs have to be considered and balanced. However, several central principles are actually fairly simple. In order to discuss and illustrate these principles in a very straightforward way, this chapter considers hiking as a metaphor for business planning.

For me, hiking involves planning and making treks in the mountains. It involves a journey with clear, long-term goals, a variety of milestones, and a team that must work together to succeed. These characteristics make hiking similar to business planning, albeit much simpler and easier to explain.

HIKING AS A PROCESS

Hiking can be viewed as a process that involves several steps or phases. This process begins by choosing a hike—deciding where you want to go. It does not make sense to start, or continue, hiking without a fairly clear notion of where you are headed. While your only goal may be an enjoyable outing, you nevertheless have to decide in which direction to head. In contrast, undirected motion happens frequently in businesses—we consider this in Chapter 5. This problem is much less likely in hiking, where the need to make a choice is very clear.

What hike should you choose? There are many, many possibilities—a taxonomy of types of hikes is discussed later. The choice among the plethora of possibilities depends on a variety of issues that are elaborated later in this chapter. Suffice it to say at this point that a choice gets made.

The next step of hiking involves "designing" the team for the hike. This includes identifying, recruiting, and training with team members. While hiking can be a solitary activity, it seldom is for me. Further, for the hiking metaphor to work in this book, consideration is limited to hiking with teams.

I have a regular hiking partner with whom I hike several times a year. I am also involved in a monthly hiking group that I lead. Thus, to an extent, you could say that the team, or teams, is set. This is often the case in business, or at least we act this way.

However, I find that the hiking team composition does vary. For example, a few years ago we hiked for a week in the Rockies. My regular partner recruited two friends to go with us who are professional guides. During the same trip, we hiked in the Cascades as part of a larger group that had paid guides.

There are about 50–60 people involved in my monthly hikes, of whom about 10–20 hike each month. Depending on how strenuous the hike is going to be, I try to make sure that particular people are part of the team. If it is going to be a relatively easy hike, I try to encourage the less fit and experienced people to be there. For a strenuous hike, where people tend to get strung out during difficult portions of the trail, I make sure that there are a few seasoned hikers on the team so we can keep track of and help the less experienced team members.

Beyond the roles of being the object or provider of mentoring and coaching, a hiking team also needs one or more people to plan and provision the hike; someone to handle maps, guidebooks, compass, and so forth; and people to lead in cooking and camping activities. If everyone tries to do everything, the workload is too great, and the results are often incoherent. Thus, a team is needed.

Most aspects of team building have complete parallels in business. Consultants may be hired when "hiking" in new markets. Easy projects may be assigned to junior team members to provide them with experiences that will prepare them for later projects. For very difficult projects, we tend to assign some of the better players because of their individual task skills and their abilities to help others. Finally, of course, tasks are partitioned among team members to balance workload and, hopefully, achieve some level of coordination.

An important issue is the training of the hiking team. There is physical training to assure that everyone is in adequate shape for the hike chosen. Often team members can do this type of training by themselves. There is also training of hiking skills, some of which is often accomplished on early, easy hikes.

Some skills such as mental endurance, however, do not come with easy hikes. These types of skills are won on trails that seem to go up forever, where a handhold is needed for every step, or when an unexpected downpour catches you without rain gear. Enduring such circumstances creates a mental toughness that enables succeeding at increasingly difficult challenges.

This is also true in business. Mortgaging your house to make payroll, and eventually tearing up the mortgage, can be a critical experience. Facing dissension and loss of confidence among your employees, and pulling the company through to a new level of success, can also be a critical experience. In this way, crises become problems needing solutions rather than catastrophes warranting panic.

With a hike chosen and a team recruited, the next step is planning the hike. This includes picking trails and determining the time and resources required. Picking trails can be straightforward. There are many guidebooks available, often with maps included and key milestones noted. Further, trails are often rated in terms of difficulty and the nature of scenery that will be experienced.

There are also many possible hikes where trails are not well documented or where trails do not really exist. In these cases, you have to discover the trail or perhaps create the trail. When the goal is very clear—for example, a summit looming in the distance—the lack of clear trails may not be a problem. However, when the goal is not clear and you are trying to make headway through vines and thickets, hiking can be discouraging and business can be exasperating.

In business, there are many possible "standard" hikes and numerous guidebooks and other forms of advice available. You need only look at existing markets, find out what they buy, and produce less expensive and perhaps better versions of these products or services. Alternatively, you can attempt to create a market for a new product or service. If your vision is clear and on target, the lack of a well-defined trail may slow you down, but you are likely to make it eventually. On the other hand, if your vision is muddled, you are very likely to get trapped by vines and thickets.

A key element of planning hikes is estimating how long the hike will take. The length of time required has a strong effect on resource requirements as discussed below. Predicting how long a hike will take involves considering the length of the hike in miles or perhaps kilometers, the elevation that will be gained, the difficulty of the terrain, and the time required for altitude accommodation or simple rest and relaxation.

With practice, you can predict the time required pretty well. Hikes on the Appalachian Trail with my usual partner require one hour for every two miles, plus whatever time we allocate for eating and basking on rock faces, taking in views. For my hiking group, I have found that we require 45 minutes to one hour per mile. Of course, if the elevation change is great and/or the terrain is very difficult, time increases. For example, a recent hike up MacRae Peak in North Carolina involved using ropes to go up steep, but not vertical, rock faces. It took three hours to hike one mile.

Another time-related issue concerns the time required for ascent versus descent. Our rule of thumb is two-thirds of the total time to get to the top and one-third to get back down. If the hike in question does not involve ascending a summit, this rule obviously is irrelevant.

Time is also a critical issue in business. Questions such as "How long will it take to get the product into the market?" and "How long before positive cash flow?" are central business planning questions. Beyond affecting resource requirements, time also can affect relative business advantages. If your company is the first business into the market with a new product, you are more likely to gain market share, profits, and so on.

My experience is that time is often more dominant than money in business planning. If the cycle time from concept to market entry is short enough, often the amount of money that can be made will easily compensate for large expenditures to achieve speed. Further, if you are really fast, you cannot spend that much money anyway—there isn't enough time for it!

The planning of hikes also involves determining what resources will be needed. Resources include fundamentals such as guidebooks, maps, a compass, and basic hiking gear—boots, clothing, and so on. The expected duration of a hike affects how much food and perhaps water will be needed and whether you will need to camp on the trail.

An important aspect of resource planning for hikes is the simple fact that whatever resources you need will have to be carried. For long hikes, the goal often becomes one of having the lightest packs possible while also having the resources that are required. This means few, if any, extras are packed "just in case." I am not suggesting that we leave the medicine kit home to save weight, but we simply make sure that the things we take are essentials.

Resource decisions in business are increasingly made the same way. Lean business processes are now the goal. Flexible systems with minimal staffing and inventories are the desired norm. This trend carries with it the important tendency to focus crisply on exactly what resources are needed to do the jobs in question. This focus can help you in both business and hiking.

Given that a destination and perhaps a trail have been chosen, a team has been recruited and trained, and a plan is prepared, the next step of hiking involves taking hikes—doing it! Issues here include making progress, dealing with setbacks, and staying on course. This seems straightforward, but a variety of factors can affect the ability of you and your team to execute your plan.

A primary element is weather. Rain probably has the greatest effect. It can make hiking a real test of character. Snow, on the other hand, is less problematic. In fact, in Georgia and North Carolina where I do most of my hiking, the temperatures are mild enough to making hiking in snow a real pleasure.

Another factor that affects progress is the trail. A trail that is in poor condition, for example, crossed by many fallen trees and/or poorly marked, can slow progress. A nonexistent trail means that you either give up or try creating your own trail—this is often termed *bushwhacking*. Before you start bushwhacking, however, it is useful to check your map and guidebook. You may be looking for the trailhead at the wrong place.

Team members can also impact your ability to progress. Injuries are obvious problems. Another common problem is people discovering that they are not in as good physical condition as they thought. A particularly difficult problem can be attitudes.

Inexperienced hikers often get discouraged. They feel hot and tired. The trail seems to go up, up, up. There may, at the moment, be no view to compensate for this investment. They may start to question whether they even like hiking. They are likely to ask for frequent breaks.

This is the type of situation where a more experie
should drop back to walk and talk with them. Tell them,
ple, that the group will hit a ridge in about one-half mil
ridge is a big rock face where they can sit in the sun for a ιew minutes and watch the hawks circling below. Then, the group will
ridge-walk for about one mile and enjoy the October sun and cool
breeze.

This kind of pep talk usually works. It gets them going again.
It also helps if you walk with them for awhile, chatting about the
flora and fauna around you, or about sports or music. This discussion distracts them from the tedium of simply putting one foot in
front of another.

It is useful to note that these tactics work even when you are
not sure where the ridge is and whether or not there is a rock face.
Simply take your best guess given the nature of the terrain where
you are hiking. If it subsequently turns out that you are wrong,
tell them that you made a mistake—you must have been remem-
bering some other trail. The point is not to deceive them. Instead,
you are teaching them about the mental attitudes they need to
develop if hiking is to become a joy rather than hours of pointless
drudgery.

The types of difficulties that impede progress in hiking also
affect businesses. The climate in the marketplace may not be as
you had assumed in your plans. The trail to market penetration
may be more difficult than you expected. And, of course, the types
of people problems that arise in hiking have perfect parallels in
business.

Despite these similarities, it often seems easier to overcome
barriers to progress in hiking than in business. I think this is due
to time scale differences. It is much easier to put up with rain and
a difficult trail for one day, than it is to weather business difficulties for months or longer. It is much easier to coach someone
through an attitude problem for the next half mile than it is to
deal with a similar problem that affects your business day after
day and week after week.

Thus far in this chapter, I have outlined the nature of hiking
and shown the parallels of the phases of hiking with those of business. For me, obviously, the metaphorical relationship between

hiking and business is compelling. In fact, I find it quite easy to think of hiking as an enterprise that is established for one day or one week with a mission, for example, to climb a particular mountain. While this argument can be made, I do not want to invoke a complex metaphor to explain a simple process. Therefore, hiking remains the metaphor and business is the reality of primary concern. The remainder of this chapter elaborates the metaphor.

DECIDING WHERE TO HIKE

Pursuit of the phases or steps of hiking depends on being able to answer the fundamental question "Where are we going?" To an extent, the answer is clear. "We are going to climb Mt. Elbert." This is a nice crisp answer with clear and auditable goals. This is one of the appealing things about hiking.

Types of Hikes

However, there are a variety of issues that you have to consider before you and your team conclude that Mt. Elbert is the hike for you. There are many types of hikes from which you can choose. Potential stakeholders—potential team members—may have very different opinions about which types of hikes are most desirable.

Types of hikes include summiting, ridge walking, and waterfalling—or, what my frequent hiking partner calls victories, vistas, and visits. There are also epics and strolls. These five types of hikes provide very different kinds of challenges and rewards.

A good example of pure summiting is climbing Mt. Elbert, the tallest mountain in Colorado. It is simply up, up, up all day. The only reason to stop along the way is to rest. At the top, the panoramic view of the Rockies is breathtaking. Getting there is a victory.

My favorite example of ridge walking is on the back side of Brasstown Bald, the tallest mountain in Georgia. While you can—perhaps unfortunately—drive up the south side of this mountain, the north side has a wonderful trail that begins at Track Rock, an archeological site known for ancient and mysterious inscriptions on three large soapstone boulders. The first mile and a half of this trail is very steep. The guidebook says that it is the toughest mile and a half in Georgia.

After this pull, you are on a ridge that has ups and downs but nothing major. For three miles or so, you hike along and criss-cross this ridge. The views are wonderful. There are several large rock faces that invite you to stretch out and enjoy being alive.

My fellow hikers and I like this ridge so much that, after the first few times, we no longer even bother to climb to the summit. We dawdle on the ridge, lay on the rock faces, and enjoy being together. The other reason we avoid the top of Brasstown Bald is the parking lot near the summit. It just doesn't seem right to cele-brate a victorious climb in a parking lot!

The most dramatic example of waterfalling I have experi-enced is Victoria Falls in Zimbabwe. The falls are absolutely awe-some. However, the hike or walk to get there is not as notable, except perhaps for the roving families of baboons. Thus, while I would love to go there again, there are examples of waterfalling that better serve our purposes in this book.

A good example is Glen Falls in North Carolina. This five- or six-mile hike starts at Little Scaly Mountain, goes around Chin-quapin, and criss-crosses the river that eventually becomes the falls. The trail follows along the descending river and provides access to four falls. You can walk out on rock faces and look up at the falls cascading down.

The power of Glen Falls compared to Victoria Falls is like a bicycle compared to a freight train. However, the intimacy possi-ble at Glen Falls is much greater, which to me is an important aspect of waterfalling. The falls at Cloudland Canyon in north-west Georgia, very close to Alabama and Tennessee, is a close sec-ond to Glen Falls in terms of this important attribute.

Epic hikes are just as the name implies. My first epic was a 2,000 mile motorcycle trip we took almost immediately after read-ing Robert Pirsig's *Zen and the Art of Motorcycle Maintenance*. While this was not a hike, our muscles felt more used and perhaps abused than they do on hikes. My first epic hike was a six-day trek along the 75-mile west coast of Holland.

The best example of an epic is the 22-mile hike from Springer Mountain, the beginning of the Appalachian Trail in Georgia, to Woody Gap. We did this hike in one day in the rain. It involved using two Jeeps, one at each end. Our wives were to drive in to the trailhead along a very rocky and muddy fire service road, pick up the second Jeep, and meet us at the other end. We would then have a victory dinner at a restaurant in Dahlonega.

Our wives got lost—fortunately not on the forest road. We shivered in our wet clothes waiting for them. Once they finally arrived, we left them at the restaurant and went to retrieve the second Jeep in the dark and thick fog. By the time we got back, the police were looking for us at our wives' behest. However, the police had not left town yet. They had started in the local bars, because their experience told them lost husbands were usually found in bars. There is more to the story, but that is enough to illustrate an epic—a hike that you take just to prove to yourselves that you can do it.

We encountered an excellent example of hikes gone awry on an earlier hike from Amicalola Falls to Springer Mountain. About one mile out from the falls, we met a fellow and his dog who were on their third day of hiking the whole Appalachian Trail from Georgia to Maine. We asked how they could be on their third day and have only covered one mile.

He said that the first day he had decided that the white blazes that mark the trail were wrong. He and his dog hiked for a whole day along some other trail, heading who knows where. At the end of the day, he realized that he was wrong. They spent the second day hiking back to Amicalola Falls. Now, the third day, they were starting again, carefully following the white blazes. I am sure that the two days they lost could easily have been avoided with a few minutes more preparation. But, the urge to get on with it, both for hikes and in business, often precludes a few minutes of planning.

The fifth type of hike is called a stroll. The best example of this, in my experience, is the Volksmarch—people's walk—in Helen, Georgia. This annual event in Georgia's piece of Bavaria involves a 12-mile hike that is very easy. Last year, our hiking team included 27 and the number of people in total was at least many hundreds. This is the type of hike where you do much chatting and little sweating or huffing and puffing. The only goal is an enjoyable day in the woods with friends.

Not all hikes fit neatly into just one cell of my taxonomy of hikes. For example, the hike from Unicoi Gap to Tray Mountain, Georgia, and back, is basically a summiting type of hike. However, for less experienced hikers, this hike tends to be an epic, because it requires three summits in one day in order to experience the wonders of being on the rock outcropping atop Tray.

I mentioned Cloudland Canyon as a waterfalling hike. It also includes a five-mile loop around the canyon that is basically a stroll. The hike from the west up Blood Mountain leads to a dramatic summit, the highest on the Appalachian Trail in Georgia. However, the first 5 to 7 miles of this 11-mile hike is more like ridge walking.

Another attribute of this taxonomy of types of hikes relates to the type of trail. For all the types of hikes, except perhaps for strolls, there are differences between following well-worn blazed trails and bushwhacking—following in others' footsteps versus creating your own trail. For the most part, I almost always use blazed trails for the simple reason that most great hiking areas have already been discovered and well used for many, many years. Another important reason for staying on blazed trails is the ecological damage you can do by wandering off trails.

A few times we have bushwhacked because we could not find the trails we were seeking. We knew where we needed to go in general, in one case a summit and in another, three waterfalls. In the first case, we ran into the trail after a mile or so. In the second, we were so drenched by rain that we never got to where we had hoped to get, although we encountered four beautiful waterfalls along the way.

To me, bushwhacking makes sense only if you have a very clear goal in mind. Then, you will know how to recognize when you have achieved it. It is similar in business. You need not have very crisp goals if you are following a standard path. In contrast, if you are trying to create a new market—bushwhacking—you need to know exactly what you are intending to accomplish.

Stakeholders' Needs and Desires

Thus, we have five types of hikes, and many hybrids, as well as the possibility of following well-worn trails or, to an extent at least, blazing our own. Potential hiking team members—the stakeholders in the hike—may have very different needs and desires with regard to the kind of hike chosen. Some people only want to "bag summits." Others seek vistas more than victories.

Within our planning framework, we can characterize differences among stakeholders' needs and desires in terms of viability, acceptability, and validity. For viability, perceptions of benefits and costs may vary. Some people may only seek accomplishments such as summits. Others may primarily enjoy the affiliation with the team.

Acceptability probably relates to whether people feel they have the abilities and resources to make a particular hike. Validity often relates to types of hikes. For example, some of the more experienced hikers in my hiking group do not feel that short, easy hikes are actually hikes at all. They want long, rigorous hikes.

This presents a dilemma in choosing hikes for the group. If all the hikes are long and rigorous, people with younger children find them unacceptable, though not invalid. Sometimes I can deal with these conflicting desires by choosing a hybrid hike that includes waterfalling, which experienced hikers still like, combined with shorter, easier trails. Other times, I don't worry about satisfying everybody.

Beyond team members' preferences, choices of hikes also depend on the experience and abilities of team members. Physical conditioning is an obvious issue. Running and walking are good ways to gain the physical endurance necessary for more difficult hikes, although some hiking techniques and skills (e.g., walking loosely rather than stiff-legged) can be gained only on hikes. Quite often people discover that they are not in good shape when they are in the middle of a trail that goes up and up. Another common discovery that people make, usually during a long and steep descent, is that they do not know how to walk in a manner that avoids jarring their knees.

While physical training can, to an extent, be accomplished running in the neighborhood or at the high school track, mental conditioning, in my opinion, is best gained on the trail. The mental side of hiking is very important for the difficult hikes where there are a few miles of upward huffing and puffing before you can catch your breath for a mile or so on a ridge, perhaps only to continue upward again for several miles to the summit.

This type of hiking requires mental toughness if it is to be rewarding. Toughness includes patience and persistence. More subtle is the mental rhythm that enables you to move on and up. I sometimes find that my mind drifts away from hiking in such situations. It doesn't seem to drift anywhere in particular, but is simply disconnected from the heavy breathing and sweating. In contrast, if I pay attention to my breath and perspiration, difficult portions of trails can seem endless.

The ability to slip, or drift, into this type of rhythm comes best with experience on difficult trails. Thus, we have taken what might be called training hikes to prepare us for a hiking trip where we expected hikes that were beyond the level of difficulty we normally experience. For instance, we regularly hiked the Appalachian Trail in Georgia in preparation for a week in the Rockies in Colorado. On these training hikes I first experienced the feeling of a mental rhythm that enabled much easier hiking on difficult sections of trails.

Competencies and Resources

Choosing hikes also depends on competencies. Knowing how to dress is one competency. The key is to dress in several layers that can be undone as you warm up and done up when you break or it gets colder. This approach to dressing is important for winter hikes. You start out all bundled up. As you start hiking, burning up the big breakfast you just had, the heat rises and you can start to unzip the windbreaker, then unsnap the down vest, then unbutton the wool sweater, and so on. Once you get really warm, you can take layers completely off and put them in your pack.

Winter hiking is my favorite. It's best when there are three to six inches of snow on the ground and all the leafless trees are coated with ice. Add a deep blue sky and bright sun. Have a temperature of about 25° to 30°F. Put it all together and you have Nirvana—a perfect way to spend a day with family, friends, and dogs.

Another competency is carrying loads. This includes arranging things in your pack so that your hips bear at least as much of the load as your shoulders. Further, you want to arrange things so that frequently needed items are readily accessible. In this way, you avoid the frustration of having to empty your entire pack, while standing in a freezing wind, to get a piece of moleskin from your medicine kit for a team member's soon-to-be blister.

A very important competency is walking. For ascents, a smooth rhythm can be created by a rocking type of movement from forward to rear legs. This is rather straightforward to learn. Descents take a bit more learning.

Most new hikers quickly get to the point of gaining only tired muscles from ascents. Descents, on the other hand, tend to produce pain, especially in the knees. What they need to learn is to loosen up and not walk so straight-legged, stiffly and consciously taking each downward step. Once they loosen up and avoid concentrating on each step, descents get much easier. I have found that it may take four to six hikes to be able to let go in this way.

In addition to competencies, there is also the issue of resources that can affect your choice of hikes. Resources include clothing, equipment, and food. Footwear is critical. Good boots— with two pairs of socks—are a joy, and bad boots can undermine everything. Beginning hikers often try to avoid buying boots. They wear heavy shoes or even athletic shoes. A frequent result is an unenjoyable hike, with very sore feet and ankles. I understand the desire to delay the investment, but unfortunately it often results in people deciding that hiking is not for them.

I earlier noted the need for layers of clothing. Fortunately, all the types of clothing that I mentioned can also be used for everyday life. Thus, this usually does not pose the same kind of investment decision. Regarding the aforementioned two pairs of socks, I usually wear a very thin pair of wick socks next to my skin and heavy wool socks over them. This keeps your feet dryer and very much decreases the opportunity for blisters.

Equipment includes packs, sleeping bags, tents, and cooking equipment. There are many guides and much expertise available to advise you on which equipment to purchase, depending on what type of hikes you intend to take. Other equipment includes knife, compass, first aid kit, maps, and trail guides. I take these items on every hike. The first aid kit gets used on every hike with my hiking group, usually for blisters and occasionally for minor cuts and scratches. My first aid kit also includes a snake-bite kit, although in the past 50 or so hikes I have seen only two snakes. The compass has come in handy a few times when, in advance, I would not have expected we would need it.

Aspirations and Expectations

Beyond competencies and resources, the choice of hikes also depends on aspirations and expectations. Hiking is best when you and your teammates share aspirations and expectations. In other words, hiking is best when there is a shared "vision" of the hike.

Hiking can be the means for pursuing a variety of aspirations. You might seek the accomplishment of summiting or the relaxation of ridge walking or waterfalling. The mental rhythm of hiking, described earlier, can also provide time to get in touch with yourself. It can also be a time to get in touch with others. And, of course, hiking provides plenty of exercise.

It is not necessary for all team members to share the exact same aspirations. It is useful, however, if the hikes chosen are compatible with the set of aspirations of team members. Thus, understanding your teammates' aspirations when hiking can be very helpful. It can enable you to focus on hiking and not be distracted by situations where the hike that you are on is not working for one or more team members. This observation is as true for business as it is for hiking.

Shared aspirations and expectations can be fostered by team-building efforts focused on creating a sense of community among team members. While there are numerous team-building exercises that might be employed, I have found that one works best— taking hikes! The challenges of hiking can provide the means for team building, particularly if you intentionally focus on the fact that you are creating and nurturing a team.

Shared meals can also facilitate team building, especially if these meals are celebrations of the team's accomplishments in hiking. By emphasizing the team's orientation toward meeting hiking challenges, as well as taking on these challenges and celebrating success, the community of hikers will come to recognize and foster their interconnectedness.

As a consequence of creating and reinforcing a sense of community, team leaders are able to focus on empowering rather than controlling team members. Leaders can become facilitators rather than commanders, leading the charge up the trail. This usually results in followers more readily communicating instead of just following. Physical and mental difficulties are more easily verbalized, and the community pitches in to help people through such potential barriers to success.

There are obvious parallels in business. Teamwork is certainly as important. The principles just described apply equally. However, what is often missing in business is the clear, concrete challenge that hiking provides. As a result, the team often lacks a concrete vision of where it is going, and it is not possible to have frequent celebrations of success because no one knows what success means. In such situations, people just keep on hiking, or maybe just shuffling along hoping that no one notices that progress is not being made. There may be much activity, but little or no progress.

The other side of aspirations is expectations. Hiking is best when your expectations are aligned with the possibilities. Hiking is often very hard work. You should expect to sweat, breathe heavily, and sometimes hurt. Progress is often slow, and the summit just ahead is frequently just a rise that leads to another rise and another. If you expect that fulfilling your hiking aspirations will be easy, you will probably be disappointed and perhaps rather frustrated.

With appropriate expectations, however, these types of difficulties will not become obstacles. For example, you will chuckle at yourself when you realize that what you thought was the summit just ahead is just a rise leading to another rise. You will chuckle because you have made this mistake many times before, and you know that you will make it many times in the future. You expect to make such mistakes.

I am not arguing that hiking should be such that your expectations are always fulfilled. Having appropriate expectations does not mean that there will not or should not be surprises. In fact, surprises are important elements of hiking—part of the adventure. I expect to be surprised! I can enjoy surprises because I am not bogged down wishing I wasn't sweaty and hoping that we will get to the top soon.

The notion of adventure reminds me of a five-day course for chief executives that I took quite a few years ago. As part of this course, the students —13 as I recall—were asked why they personally were in business. There were many standard answers including money, power, and accomplishment.

I had only one thing to add beyond what everyone else said. I added adventure as one of the reasons that I am in business. The course leader asked if I meant risk. I said that risk might capture what I meant. Then he wrote on the board "minimize risk."

I immediately responded that I did not want risk minimized. In fact, I like it that there are risks. I highly value the challenge of dealing with risks and the excitement of succeeding, as well as the lessons of failing. Business is an adventure for me, as is hiking. I like it that way.

This does not mean that adventure should be one of the benefits that everybody seeks from hiking or business. I offer it simply as an example of the roles that aspirations and expectations can play relative to choosing hikes. In Chapters 6 and 7, the process of discovering what drives you is pursued in depth.

Summarizing briefly, in the last few pages I have elaborated the question, "Where are we going?" There are many types of hikes that might be chosen. The choices depends on stakeholders' preferences, as well as on their competencies, resources, aspirations, and expectations. In this way, choosing what hike to take is similar to choosing what business to pursue. These parallels are further discussed in Chapter 5.

DECIDING HOW TO HIKE

Beyond the question of what hike to take, there is the question of how to take it. "Bagging summits" is not the essence of hiking any more than distributing year-end bonuses is the essence of being in business. The real payoff in hiking is the process.

The process of hiking is rife, literally, with ups and downs. Just as in business, you cannot eliminate all difficulties—you learn to anticipate and manage them. Further, while things may be going great now, you do not feel that you've made it and will never face difficulties again.

Occasionally, a mile or two of ridge walking makes hiking almost effortless. But, fortunately, ridges do not last forever. Eventually, you head upward again. In your upward climb, you inevitably encounter false summits—what appear to be the top of the mountain until you get there and realize that the summit is beyond. False summits can, nevertheless, be minor victories on the path to the summit. Although, once you get to the summit, you invariably will see other appealing summits in the distance.

As noted earlier, choosing trails requires deciding between well-worn trails where you do not need a map or compass and new trails where you have to pay careful attention. At an extreme, you could choose to drive up Brasstown Bald, Clingmans Dome, or Mt. Mitchell—the tallest mountains in Georgia, Tennessee, and North Carolina, respectively—or you could choose to climb more obscure trails where much more effort is needed.

New or infrequently used trails present several risks. You might become lost or misplaced. You are lost when you do not know where you are. You are misplaced when you know exactly where you are, but it's the wrong place. We have very seldom been lost. However, we have been misplaced when we took little-used and poorly marked trails and discovered an hour or two later that we were on a different trail, headed to a different destination, than we had planned. Sometimes the new destination was more appealing than the original one. In most cases, we had to retrace our steps, which is not all that bad if you enjoy the process of hiking.

While new trails can be more difficult and occasionally confusing, they also can present the possibility of large returns. By breaking new ground, you can gain new views. By following seldom-used trails, you can experience summits, ridges, or waterfalls that are more like the wilderness than are popular trails. You can gain the experience of what it might have been like before there were well-established trails.

There are similar choices in business. You can attempt to enter existing markets, perhaps with a higher-quality and/or lower-priced product or service. In contrast, you can attempt to identify emerging market needs that are not being filled and try, perhaps via new technologies, to quickly become the market leader. There are, of course, many hybrid strategies between these two extremes, just as there are many hikes between the extremes of hiking on well-worn trails and bushwhacking.

Process planning for a hike involves choosing a trail, as well as the aforementioned estimation of time requirements and the consequent provisions needed. A more subtle aspect of this process planning concerns the pacing and rhythm of the hike. Pacing and rhythm are crucial to enjoying hiking, especially in adverse conditions.

Rain is my least favorite adverse condition, unless it is just a light mist. Snow is great although, as I noted earlier, this preference is probably highly biased by my hiking being predominantly in areas where three to six inches of snow is a big deal. One can easily prepare for cold. Ice can make progress very slow, unless you have the right equipment.

On the other end of the scale, I have found hot sun and/or high humidity to be more difficult. The colder it gets, the more layers you put on. The hotter it gets, the more layers you take off. But you reach a limit. Nude hiking is not that much fun, especially through brambles, over fallen tree trunks, and up big rock formations. And you still have to carry a pack, with all those layers you have taken off.

Evolutionary Hiking

I have found a way to deal with adverse conditions that works for me. In Chapter 3, the concept of evolutionary product families was introduced and discussed. This concept can be transformed to what I call evolutionary hiking. The family of hikes that results includes Levels A, B, and C.

Level C is the Ultimate Hike, the meaning of which differs for victories, vistas, or visits. Level C might, for example, be captured by the vision of yourself on top of the summit that you are attempting to climb in the next two or three days. Level A could be the next 100 steps or the path to the top of the next rise. Level B might be the hike ending at lunch break or at the end of the day.

With this construct in mind, all you have to do right now is Level A. Your overriding goal is to accomplish the next 100 steps. That's all. The other hikes—Levels B and C—will evolve from succeeding in this and in subsequent 100-step hikes.

The value of this construct is very evident when you are trudging along at 14,000+ feet. The grade is difficult, breathing is tough, and the sun in blazing. The top seems very far away. But that next rise—if it were the top you could make it easily. Pretend it is the top and slowly make your way to it. Look around and enjoy the view. Now look for the next milestone about 100 steps away.

My frequent hiking partner uses a somewhat different approach in such situations. He focuses on the immediate surroundings and forgets about the need to get somewhere. In this way, his Level A is very immediate and only requires being on the trail.

With mental games such as these, you can enable yourself to accomplish things that on the surface appear daunting. For example, you have a grand vision (Level C) for a new product that will create a totally new market. Your business planning leads to a very much toned down and easily created version (Level A) of this product. You set out to create this product and get it into the market, expecting only very modest success initially but knowing that your subsequent product (Level B) has much greater potential.

With such a plan in hand, most of your energy goes into Level A. Your competitors see a modest product that penetrates the market in a fairly modest way. They may choose to imitate what you offer with a fast follow. But that's okay, because some of your energy is focused on Level B, which will be far superior to your Level A as well as to their imitations.

The vision (Level C) is the reason you are on the trail, but Level A and, to an extent, Level B are what guide your next steps. Further, the celebration for reaching Level A—for example, a break, drink of water, and a view—is what keeps you going. The excitement of migrating elements of the former Level B to the new Level A is what gets you going again. It is a mental game, but it works.

Lessons Learned

I do not mean to imply that you can avoid all frustrations and setbacks. Sometimes things do not work out as you hoped. A few years ago, we were trying to increase my then 8 -ear-old daughter's enthusiasm for hiking. Up until then she had decided that hiking was boring.

We made great progress when we climbed Mt. Pisgah in North Carolina. Mt. Pisgah is a fairly short hike with very clear goals. You can see the summit from the trailhead. My daughter was the first to the top. She and all of us enjoyed lunch on a large rock outcropping on the summit. We had kindled some real enthusiasm.

We decided that we could accomplish another climb that afternoon. We chose nearby Richland Balsam. This hike managed to dampen all our spirits. After an hour or so of hiking through the woods, we reached a small clearing, surrounded by large trees, that had a small wooden sign, "Richland Balsam: Summit." My daughter asked, "Is this it? That's all there is?" She and the rest of us had no sense of accomplishment.

The lack of a "real" summit would have been acceptable had we walked an interesting ridge or paused at appealing waterfalls. However, this hike had none of these features. Nevertheless, the hike was not a complete waste. I learned an important lesson about selecting hikes for the family and other groups. I try to make sure that there is some prize in terms of summits, ridges, or waterfalls. I save epics for diehards like myself and a few other aficionados.

Another hike that did not turn out as hoped was Mt. Rainier in the Cascades in the state of Washington. This three-day effort included one day of training to work with a roped team and to walk on ice with crampons. The second day involved hiking up to a tiny lodge at 10,000 feet where we slept until a very early morning ascent to the summit at 14,000+ feet.

All went well for me until the portion of the hike approaching a resting point at 12,300 feet. I had great difficulty with the ropes. The goal is to keep the rope from becoming too slack between you and the person in front of you. Consequently, if the person in front of you slows down or stops, you have to do the same. If that person speeds up you have to speed up.

As a result of this relationship between you and the person in front of you, your pace is entirely determined by another person. If you hit an easy stretch, you cannot speed up because the rope will slacken. If the other person hits an easy stretch while you are still struggling on the incline he or she just left, that person may speed up and, via the rope, pull you down. Of course, an experienced team would not do this. But, with the exception of our guide, we all had roughly one day of experience.

By the time we reached 12,300 feet, I was exhausted. I had been pulled down repeatedly and could not get into any rhythm. The guide told me that I should rest at this point while the team continued on up. I did not like this idea, but I knew he was right.

I crawled into a sleeping bag and watched the sun rise. Why had I failed? The previous week I had climbed a mountain higher than Rainier. Thus, it wasn't simply the altitude. It was clearly my inability to deal with the dynamics of being roped to my team members.

In the two hours that I waited for my team to return, I reflected on this inability. It struck me that I seldom if ever place myself in situations where my pace is totally determined by out-side forces. I am not very good at tasks where I cannot work ahead and create a cushion for times when the pace exceeds my abilities.

I made a discovery. I discovered more about myself and how I approach work. I learned how these tendencies help me with some types of work and hinder me with others. I also learned about how I pace myself, which until then I had not realized.

Discoveries about yourself, as well as about the world in general, are discussed in Chapters 6 and 7. Thus, these lessons need not be elaborated here. It is important to note, however, that my failure to reach the summit of Mt. Rainier was a success in terms of understanding myself better.

Another example of hikes not going quite as expected happened on Red Peak in the Colorado Rockies. This hike was part of my first backpacking trip. Until then I had only carried a day pack. On that trip I learned how to carry a full pack.

On the second day out, we summited Red Peak at 13,000+ feet and were headed down the opposite side. We came to a narrow ledge that our guides scampered quickly around. I was next. I was staring at the sheer drop over the edge. It seemed very, very far down—in reality, my guess is that it was a few hundred feet.

One guide hailed me to come on along. He said, "It's easy." I knew that I was not yet very sure-footed carrying my pack. I lacked confidence in my ability to make it. I turned to the second guide, "I'd like a second opinion." She smiled and showed me several handholds that would enable me to not have to depend solely on my ability to balance myself and my pack. I made it through. I accomplished something I would never have expected I could do nor even have attempted.

After I made it by this ledge, we had to work our way down between two rock faces to get to a more level hiking area. I made it easily with my newfound confidence. However, as I got to the bottom, my pants split completely from below my zipper all the way around to my belt in the back. They split loudly and completely. Everyone had a good laugh at the rookie. So did I.

Some lessons are more subtle. As part of a business meeting in Los Alamos, New Mexico, we decided to take a hike. We could have the same discussions on the trail that we could have had in a meeting room. As an aside, I have had many business meetings on hikes. It provides a great venue for wrestling with tough problems and difficult decisions.

For this hike, we started at the plateau surrounding Los Alamos and hiked down to the Rio Grande. The last half of the hike, obviously, involved hiking back up. It was snowing as we made the ascent. The canyon scenery in the falling snow was wonderful.

What struck me most about this hike, however, was that it ended in an ascent. I had never hiked before where the second half was much more work than the first half. It had always been the other way around. Of course, there is no inherent reason that hikes should be one way or another. I realized that one of my unspoken beliefs about hikes was faulty.

From a more practical point of view, I realized that the way I usually pace myself on hikes is premised on an up-then-down sequence. My usual way of allocating both my physical and mental energies is premised on this sequence. The Los Alamos hike helped me to understand the implicit assumptions I had been making. A subtle lesson, but an important one, that later helped me during a much more rigorous hike in the Grand Canyon. This type of phenomenon is further discussed in Chapters 6 and 7.

RELATIONSHIPS

It should be very clear from the numerous vignettes I have thus far related that relationships are central to hiking. One set of relationships involves your hiking partners. Walking and climbing with people for 10 to 12 hours per day, and perhaps camping with them at night, provides much opportunity to talk about virtually everything. The aforementioned sense of community can be greatly enhanced by such opportunities.

Hiking, like business, is best viewed as a team effort. Thus, a central relationship issue concerns the roles of team members. One role involves planning the hike, including reviewing guidebooks, obtaining maps, coordinating transportation, and checking on weather. Another role is concerned with equipment and provisions, either by specifying what each team member should bring or by obtaining items directly.

During the hike, there are two or more leadership roles. One involves who is in front watching for blazes and keeping an eye out for double blazes, which indicate changes of direction, including switchbacks. Another leadership role is usually filled by somebody at the back who makes sure that everyone is there, encourages stragglers, and coaches novices. If cooking and/or camping is involved, two other roles involve food preparation/ cleanup and making/breaking camp.

All of these roles can be filled by one person, perhaps a very experienced hiker or a paid guide. However, it is more common for the roles to be distributed among team members, and perhaps changed, depending on the circumstances. For instance, I often lead my hiking group for the first mile or so, but usually shift to a role farther back in the pack as we progress. This makes it easier to spot people having trouble and provide them with some encouragement. Several people in this group provide leadership in terms of keeping the group together psychologically.

Teams do not necessarily inherently work well together. Some training is often very useful. Earlier I mentioned the use of team-building exercises. For example, a popular exercise involves getting everyone to stand on a four-by-four timber in random order, and then having them rearrange themselves in alphabetical order without talking and without falling off. This exercise clearly demonstrates the need for cooperation.

However, I think that team training is better done in the context in which the team has to perform. In this way, not only will team members gain an appreciation for the need to cooperate— they will develop some skill in doing it in the context in which it will be needed. Thus, in my experience, the best way to train a hiking team is to take them on hikes.

This approach to training sounds much easier than it is. You cannot simply take people on hikes and assume that they will gain the team skills they need. The training aspect of the hikes has to be intentional. You have to decide which people need which skills, provide them opportunity and instruction in these skills, and coach them as they progress. In this way, people develop the skills needed, albeit slowly sometimes, while also enjoying what they want to do in the first place—hike.

Another set of relationships is with you tools of hiking. Without the right equipment, hiking can be undermined. Inadequate hiking b est woe. Bulky inappropriate clothing can be b and uncomfortable, as well as potentially danger

On the other hand, the "goodness" of your equipment does not mean you can avoid the normal pangs of hiking. Packs are still heavy. Feet and boots still tire of each other. Nevertheless, you cannot afford to let your relationship with your pack and boots sour. The care of your equipment is central to your success.

Yet another set of relationships is with the trail. Few interesting and rewarding trails are flat and smooth. The breathtaking view from the summit is gained, obviously, by climbing up, up, up. Trails that seem to go up forever are part of reaching the top.

The rocks and roots in the trail that make walking difficult are simply the way that nature is put together. At times it may seem that trails conspire to sap your energy and catch the toes of your boots. However, trails also wear and fail under the pounding of your feet.

In all of these relationships, a key distinction is between control and collaboration. We have a tendency to feel that we have to be in control, using equipment, trails, and sometimes people to achieve our ends. We tend to want to own equipment, master trails, and to an extent have power over people.

Hiking is better if we overcome these tendencies and relinquish control. We need to collaborate with equipment and trails, just as we need to collaborate with wood and tools. Similarly, we need to collaborate in business planning and in product planning. Collaboration involves working with people and things to pursue common goals, rather than trying to maintain control and make people and things pursue your goals.

Hiking provides, I think, an excellent metaphor for business. However, hiking is also an experience in itself. My passions for hiking extend far beyond its value as a way to think about my business and the businesses of those I help.

Difficult hikes can provide an element of passion. There is a genderless sexuality that emerges with a hard climb to an expansive, sun-drenched rock face overlooking the mountain range, with hawks circling below. There is a wonderful feeling of being spent and luxuriating in the sun and wind.

There is a different kind of passion related to being part of re. There is a sense of wonder at feeling small but not insignificant because you are an integral part of the dense woods, towering rocks, and thundering waterfalls. There is a sense that all is right with the world.

I also am passionate about winter hikes. This feeling is strongest when all the trees are encased in ice, outlined against the blue, blue sky and reflecting the bright sun in every faceted limb. Hiking in such surrounds is like being in a fantasy.

Passions such as just described provide a sense of yourself and your relationships with the cosmos. They provide a means for continual discovery. We return to this topic in Chapters 6 and 7.

HIKING AS A METAPHOR

It is relatively easy to illustrate a variety of business-planning concepts and principles in the context of hiking. Hiking is a straightforward, goal-oriented activity pursued by teams whose members have multiple roles. However, hiking does not capture several aspects of business planning that are very important.

Most businesses are not as single-minded as a typical hiking team can be. In effect, most businesses are simultaneously pursuing multiple hikes of different types. Sales and marketing's emphasis on closing deals is akin to always trying to summit. Engineering's pursuit of the wonders of technology is similar to waterfalling. Manufacturing, when trying to meet heavy production demands, may often feel it is on an epic. Top management may, in its visionary role, be ridge walking.

The range of perspectives across functional areas in an enterprise leads to much more complex organizational problems than can be addressed within the simple metaphor of hiking. We need to consider explicitly the hierarchy of goals, strategies, and plans within an enterprise and how different functions can and should contribute. These relationships are considered in Chapter 5.

On a hike it is usually very clear if you are progressing toward your goal. It is much more difficult to make this assessment in business. It is much easier to get lost or misplaced in business than in hiking. Thus, we need some means to plan and measure progress. While sales, cash flow, and profits are good measures, they are inadequate for processes that evolve over long periods of time and only lead to monetary rewards if things done much earlier were done right. An approach to dealing with this issue is discussed in Chapter 5.

Business is also much more difficult than hiking in terms of assessing in advance the likely success of a plan. This is due in part to the greater complexity of the business undertaking. It is also due to the nature of competitive forces—there are people who would like to thwart your "hiking" plans. Chapter 5 discusses the problem of assessing likely success.

Business planning should deal with the basic issues raised in this chapter in the context of hiking. However, beyond these issues, business planning also needs to consider the complexities of cross-functional planning, the dynamics of planning and execution, and the factors likely to underlie success in a typically complex, competitive environment. The methodologies discussed in this book provide you a means for pursuing all of these issues in an integrated and straightforward manner.

How good of a metaphor for business is hiking? It seems to me that hiking captures a variety of organizational issues very well, particularly people-related issues. Further, because it is so concrete, it clearly illustrates why the planning of journeys is important. In fact, if more enterprises saw themselves on journeys, the metaphor of hiking would be even more applicable and enterprises would tend to have better plans.

Woodworking helped us to understand market-oriented product planning and design. Hiking helped us to understand the importance of the organization in terms of its internal stakeholders' preferences, competencies, resources, aspirations, and expectations. Further, we considered how these factors affect the journey chosen, as well as how it is taken.

Now, we need to place this organization and its products in the marketplace. The collaborative team with its potentially delightful products must deal with a variety of competitors and competitive forces. In Chapter 5, these types of issues are pursued in depth.

5

Business
Planning

The euphoria of creation usually
prevents inventors from perceiving
the prerequisites for market innovations.

In this chapter, the discussion moves from the specifics of hiking to the generalities of business planning. This continues my overall plan to first illustrate concepts and principles in concrete, relatively simple domains. The discussion is then broadened and abstracted to include all aspects of the type of planning being considered. Finally, the generalized set of concepts and principles is illustrated in the context of a detailed case study.

It is important to begin by differentiating product plans from business plans. Your product plans should be oriented toward creating a new or improved product, system, or service. Your business plans should focus on competing and succeeding in the marketplace.

INVENTION VERSUS INNOVATION

How are these different? Product plans may involve invention—creation of a new device or process. Business plans, in contrast, should focus on innovation—creation of change via something new. While market innovations may rely on one or more inventions, the essence of innovation is not invention.

The vast majority of inventions never result in business success. The vast majority of patents never lead to business success. Put simply, most new devices or processes do not result in anybody changing.

What changes should you seek? The change you want is for people to buy your products and services, vote for your platform, and so on. You want them to change from their previous way of doing things and adopt your way. You want them to change from buying from some other company and buy from you. This is the essence of market innovation.

Why do inventions so seldom succeed? My experience is that the problem is a lack of intention to succeed. Inventors tend to focus on the elegance, simplicity, power, and so forth, of their designs. Their measures of success are very local. They get the device or process to work. They determine that they have the technically correct solution to the problem they have chosen to address.

One of our customers recently gave me a cartoon that depicts a jubilant scientist who has succeeded in creating a process that transforms pocket lint to artificial parsley. His boss asks him what the company should do with this invention. The scientist replies that that isn't his problem. His only job is to be technically correct.

Inventors are seldom innovators because that is not their intention. Consequently, they pay little if any attention to how to create change. They seldom concern themselves with the prerequisites for convincing the marketplace to change. As a result, many if not most, of their creations are not perceived by the market to be viable, acceptable, and valid.

Chapter 3 focused on how to assure that products, systems, and services score well on these dimensions. Using the product planning and design methodology described in that chapter can be an important step toward market innovations. The next step involves creating an appropriate organization for designing, developing, manufacturing, marketing, selling, and servicing these potential innovations.

MISSION AND VISION

The nature of the organization should be driven by what the enterprise is trying to accomplish in the marketplace. What relationship with the marketplace do you seek? What type of hike do you want to take?

You might try summiting with a goal of becoming the next Microsoft, Home Depot, or Toys 'R Us, with dramatic increases in sales and market presence. Alternatively, you might pursue ridge walking with a clear view of where you might get many years from now and steady but modest increases in sales and profits. Yet another alternative is the boutique, specialty business such as an R&D think tank or fine woodworking, both of which are akin to waterfalling and enjoying the wonders of technologies, mahoganies, and so on.

There are very few strolls in business and many, many epics. I have heard the typical epic referred to as the "walking dead." Every month, making payroll is a worry, creditors are kept at bay, and once in a while your cash flow catches up for a week or two. Then, it's back to hanging on by your fingernails.

I do not know what percentage of businesses are stuck in epic hikes. Our company and I imagine most companies have once or twice experienced aspects of being on an epic hike. While these experiences are said to build character—and I am inclined to believe this—epics are not the type of experience for which one is likely to volunteer.

Perhaps the best way to weather an epic is to clearly know where you are headed. For example, if an epic is a necessary step in getting to the summit, ridge, or waterfall that is part of your vision, then you can prepare for and endure the epic much better. Thus, an important element of survival and sanity concerns knowing where you are going.

Two constructs are usually invoked as means to characterize goals of enterprises: mission and vision. Many enterprises have mission statements. Frequently, these statements are glittering generalities such as "quality for our customers." It is difficult to argue with this, but it does not provide a sense of direction.

I think that a mission statement should answer the four questions listed in Figure 5.1. In other words, what is the enterprise's value added in the marketplace, who gets this value added, and how is this value added provided?

Who:	Who are the beneficiaries of the enterprise's activities?
Where:	Where can they be found, e.g., in market sectors?
What:	What benefits are they provided by the enterprise?
How:	How are these benefits provided?

Figure 5.1   Elements of a Mission Statement

It is important to emphasize the philosophy underlying these questions. The purpose of an enterprise is to provide benefits, to provide value added. These benefits and value added should be considered from the point of view of the enterprise's stakeholders, particularly customers and users, but also employees, investors, and so forth. If the enterprise focuses on being very good at providing benefits and value added, this enterprise is likely to enjoy substantial sales and profits.

In contrast, if the enterprise chooses sales and profits as its primary goals, it is less likely to succeed. You can go into the bakery business to make a lot of money, or you can go into the bakery business to put quality baked goods in people's hands at an attractive price. You will make much more money in the latter case than in the former.

Thus, I am advocating a totally market-driven approach to business planning. You should be driven by the market's current and anticipated needs, desires, and preferences. This is true for businesses, educational institutions, government agencies, and so on.

This is less straightforward than it sounds. Many potential new products and services are such that the market has not "asked" for them. The market may not even know that such offerings exist or are possible. In such situations, you need to be very close to customers using the methods and tools discussed in Chapter 3.

Therefore, being market driven does not mean that you provide only what is explicitly requested. What it means is that your planning is dominated by the market's interests. If you understand these interests deeply, you may be able to provide new products and services that will "delight" the market even though they had no expectations of such delights.

While the mission of the enterprise should be market driven, the vision of the enterprise's future should have both external and internal components. The external vision relates to the role, image, and position of the enterprise in the markets it serves and plans to serve. Using a ship metaphor, the external vision is the anticipated view from the bridge.

The internal vision is the view in the engine room. Employees in particular not only want to know where the ship is going and what sights will be seen—they also want to know what it will be like onboard. What is the likely work environment? What jobs will there be and what skills will they require? What will be the pay levels and benefits? The internal vision has to answer these types of questions and answer them acceptably for people to buy into the enterprise's mission and external vision.

This is due to the fact that not everyone in the enterprise is on the same hike, or at least not on the hike for the same reason. Some people have their eyes on the summit, and the mission to get there will sufficiently compel them. Others find the ridges rewarding whether or not any summits are reached. They want to know what the hike will be like along the way, not just at the summit. Similarly, the waterfallers will want to know, for example, if particular technologies will be central to getting to the summit. They are less concerned with the summit than they are that they get to learn about and use these technologies.

The combination of mission, external vision, and internal vision can provide the means for portraying all aspects of the hike. Different people will value different aspects of these portrayals. The key is to get everyone to find sufficient value to be willing to commit themselves to the whole package. To the extent that there is a sense of community in the enterprise, people are likely to be willing to commit to aspects of the package that they do not personally value but they understand are important to other members of the community.

I frequently am asked about how you can know if you have chosen the "right" mission and vision. My answer is that you cannot be right or wrong in this choice. It, quite simply, is a choice based on needs, beliefs, and perceptions. There is no right or wrong, other than perhaps from an ethical perspective.

However, there are good and bad choices. A good choice is one where you subsequently work out a plan for pursuing the chosen mission and vision. The resulting plan seems reasonable and you can confidently implement it. While this does not guarantee success, it is nevertheless a "good" choice.

In contrast, a bad choice of mission and vision is such that you have no plan or a poor plan for pursuing them. Perhaps you have a good plan—at least the best plan possible—that shows you cannot reasonably expect to make progress in pursuing the chosen mission and vision. In such situations, if you continue with this choice, it's a "bad" choice.

Given an initial choice of mission and vision, the next question concerns how to pursue these summits, ridges, or waterfalls. The first step in answering this question involves identifying core competencies necessary to this pursuit. What specific knowledge and skills are needed in engineering, manufacturing, marketing, sales, service, finance, and so on? Which of these competencies are your strong suits? Which will you have to augment? At this point, you can answer these questions in a fairly qualitative manner. Once markets, products, technologies, and so forth, are defined, you should reconsider these questions in more detail.

It may seem odd to many readers that I advocate choosing your mission and vision without first considering your competencies. My reasons for this are quite straightforward. First, my experience has been that enterprises seldom wander very far away from their core competencies. Their failure to make good choices is not due to a lack of relevance of their existing competencies. Failures are more often due to not recognizing the additional competencies that will be needed in order to succeed.

Second, I have found that "backing into" a mission and vision from existing competencies often leads to a survivalist mentality. What can we do to use our existing engineering expertise and facilities? How about building widgets? Great, that's settled. Let's get on with it!

This scenario has two flaws. How do we know that we can compete in the widget market? Does anybody buy widgets now? If not, why not? If so, why will the other players let us in?

A more important flaw is the way in which "backing in" distorts the purpose of the mission and vision. By backing in, you are saying, in effect, that the mission is to use existing competencies. The vision is to be like we have always been. This approach represents enterprise-centered planning, *not* market-driven planning. This approach assumes that the purpose of the market is to meet your needs, rather than embracing the tenet that your purpose is to meet the market's needs.

PRODUCT AREAS AND PLANS

Once needed competencies have been identified and assessed, the next question concerns product offerings. By "product" I mean off-the-shelf products, systems built to order, and services that are sold as ends in themselves. Thus, for example, an educational program can be viewed as a product sold to students. Corporate R&D can be viewed as a product sold to operating units.

New ventures may have only a single product that they hope to offer the market. However, most enterprises have multiple offerings. It is important to consider how these offerings can be clustered or organized in some manner.

Dimensions along which product offerings can be clustered include market relationships, product linkages, underlying technologies, and facility requirements. Products are clustered in terms of market relationships because they sell in the same or related markets. Product linkages are used to cluster products that tend to sell together. Clustering in terms of underlying technologies makes sense if customers are aware of these technologies, and these technologies govern their purchasing decisions. Clustering around, for example, manufacturing facilities might be used if sales are inherently localized as they are for chains of retail stores or restaurants.

The process of clustering yields one or more product areas. It is important that these areas be defined from the perspective of the marketplace. There is a tendency to organize relative to internal processes. Thus, for example, we might have one plan for selling widgets and another for selling maintenance of widgets. We might group all the product offerings in one area and all the maintenance service offerings in another area. However, this is not the way that customers think about their widgets or their other purchases. They expect one-stop shopping for their widget needs. Therefore, widget maintenance services should be part of the overall widget plan.

Market:	Nature of market needs, purchase transactions, and competition
Product:	Market-oriented characterization of the product, system, or service
Technology:	Underlying elements of product, system, or service
Manufacturing:	Means of creating and delivering product, system, or service
Services:	Activities supporting sales and use of product, system, or service
R&D:	Creation of new elements for future versions of product, system, or service

Figure 5.2   Elements of a Product Plan

Organizing the enterprise's plans from customers' perspectives has important implications. The functional "stovepipes" that often arise and become institutionalized have no value for the customer. Rather than have an engineering plan, a manufacturing plan, a finance plan, and so on, it makes much more sense for all plans to be cross-functional and to have elements of each function's goals, strategies, and activities represented within them.

From this point of view, all plans have to "make sense" to customers. If customers could not *potentially* understand the value that a particular activity provides them, this activity is suspect. If customers, perhaps with a bit of education, could not understand the value of a plan, this plan is suspect. I am not arguing that such activities and plans should be automatically eliminated. I am suggesting, however, that customer-oriented audits of activities and plans can provide very useful insights.

Within each product area, one or more product plans can be developed. Each plan includes the six primary sections listed in Figure 5.2. In addition, there is consideration of risks and unknowns within each of these six areas. Note that I have repeatedly used the phrase "product, system, or service" to emphasize the broad and inclusive meaning that I attach to the word "product." Henceforth, I will just use this single word.

These six sections can be thought of in a hierarchical manner. Market needs determine the nature of the product and its underlying technology. These two elements, in turn, determine goals for manufacturing, services, and R&D. Thus, a four-level strategic hierarchy emerges, including:

- Mission

- Product Areas

- Products—defined by markets and enabled by technologies

- Manufacturing, Services, and R&D

Defining this hierarchy across the enterprise and completing each of the elements of each plan constitute the essence of strategic business planning. We now need to elaborate the nature of each of the six elements of each plan.

STRATEGIC PLANNING

As shown in Figure 5.3, strategic planning starts with consideration of the market. Much of the information needed to characterize the market will have been gained during the naturalist and marketing phases of the product planning process. The focus at this point is on what the market needs and wants.

MARKET

- What benefits will our product provide?

- Who wants these benefits?

- How many people want these benefits?

- How will the product be purchased?

- How much will people be willing to pay?

- How much revenue can we expect?

PRODUCT

- What specific functionality will be provided?

- How will this functionality provide the desired benefits?

- What are the competing approaches to providing these benefits?

- Why will the competition let us succeed?

- What will be the total costs of competing?

TECHNOLOGY

- How will the product functionality be realized?

- What competitive advantage do we have?

- What unknowns remain?

- What are the risks?

Figure 5.3 Strategic Planning Questions

The first market question is "What benefits will our product provide?" A fairly common answer is "Customers will get my product." This answer describes the benefits that *you* will get—sales of your product—not necessarily what the customer wants.

To answer this question appropriately, you have to step away from your product and ask why people would buy it. For example, people buy the planning tools discussed in Chapter 3 because they want good plans quickly, not because they inherently want software tools. They want the benefits of having the tools, not the tools in themselves.

This distinction has important implications. One of the large defense companies with whom I have worked was developing plans to diversify from its traditional defense markets. They were considering alternative outlets for, in their case, guns and bullets. They discussed police forces and sportsmen. However, they were hard-pressed to imagine sufficient replacement markets for their declining defense sales.

Focusing squarely on the benefits question, we came to realize that customers, even military customers, do not particularly want guns and bullets. Historically, they bought rocks, and then spears, and eventually bows and arrows, and more recently guns and bullets. They did not want any of these things. They want destructive force that enables them to control situations either by threat of use of force or actual use of force.

This company realized that they are in the destructive-force business. This led them to consider the alternative markets for destructive force, as well as the alternative means of providing destructive force. Their subsequent vision—Level C—of their eventual product line is very different from what it might have been without this realization.

Another mid-sized company with whom I worked was developing plans for growing its offerings in materials-testing services. One of the types of tests, for example, involves testing samples as a basis of predicting the likely life of metal parts that are subject to high temperatures and frequent reversal of stresses, which can lead to phenomena called creep and fatigue, respectively. Their concern was with how to increase the market for these tests.

The benefits question led us to consider why people buy tests. Is it because they inherently value tests? The answer is obvious. What they want is test results. Why? They want to be confident in the life of their parts. Thus, the real benefit is confidence, not tests.

This realization led this company to quickly conclude that they had much more competition than they had thought. They were readily able to name four distinct ways to provide the confidence sought by customers, one of which is computational and does not involve testing. This also led this company to conclude that they had the competencies and the resources to provide confidence in more than the one way they had been employing. Thus, they realized that they had more competition, but they also realized that they had more options.

A fairly recent effort involved helping a company plan a new product family of sensors. One type of sensor nonobtrusively senses the levels of liquids in tanks of dangerous and/or toxic chemicals. In this case, the pursuit of the benefits question led to the conclusion that customers do not want to know "how high"—they want to know "how much." As a consequence of this conclusion, this company realized that there were more ways to address this problem than they had envisioned.

The next market question is "Who wants these benefits?" Is it, for example, doctors, lawyers, or Indian chiefs? The answer to this question is highly influenced by how benefits have been framed.

For instance, one large aerospace company with whom I have worked had developed a software tool for assessing visibility and reachability in aircraft cockpits. When we started to look at the market for this tool, the problem was first stated in terms of finding additional customers for the cockpit design tool. Framing the question in this way quickly led to the conclusion that the three or four cockpit design organizations in this company were the only customers for this tool.

Fortunately, we recast the problem as one of finding customers for a visibility and reachability analysis tool. This got us out of the cockpit and into maintenance, manufacturing, and so on. As I recall, we readily produced a list of 30–40 organizations whose problems were addressable with this tool.

The next question is, "How many people want these benefits?" In other words, what is the size of the market? The answer should, if possible, address both the market that is currently served and the potential market.

This question can be answered in several ways. There is a wide variety of databases of demographic information available that can, for instance, tell you how many companies are within each Standard Industry Code (SIC). There are also databases that can tell you where people live, what jobs they hold, how much money they make, and how they currently spend it. It is also, of course, possible to perform or commission market studies.

Given an understanding of the benefits sought, who wants them, and how many of these types of people there are, the next concern is getting the product to them. The question is "How will the product be purchased?" This seems straightforward. You put the product on the shelf, people buy it, and you get the money.

However, very few purchases are that simple. How will you get the product on the shelves? Whose shelves? If not yours, then how will you convince others to put your product on their shelves? Once they are convinced, how will the products get there? Whose trucks, trains, or planes will be used? If not yours, then how much will transportation cost, and how timely and reliable are the alternative modes of transportation?

The general issue here is marketing, distribution, and sales. This issue is often discussed in terms of channels from producers to consumers. You might sell directly to customers via your own sales force. You might sell to retail stores, perhaps via distributors, who then sell to customers. You might sell to original-equipment manufacturers who include your product as a component in their equipment systems. You might sell to value-added resellers who package your product with, for example, customized services that they then sell directly to customers. There are many alternatives.

One of the best ways to determine what channels might work best is to ask potential customers how they currently get their products and services. In addition, you might ask questions related to the level of satisfaction they experience with these channels. A lack of satisfaction might provide an opportunity. Questions related to existing channels and customers' satisfaction with them can be incorporated into the naturalist and marketing phases of the product-planning and design process.

Beyond the choice of channels, there is the issue of how to get people's attention. Advertising and promotions are standard approaches. Marketing via seminars and publications are common approaches, particularly for products that require educated customers. Identifying and contacting customers via referrals from existing customers tends to result in very solid sales leads.

While it is impossible to discuss in the confines of this chapter all possible approaches to marketing, distribution, and sales, it is very important to understand the central importance of this issue. Getting potential customers' attention and efficiently getting products to them is crucial if sales expectations are to be met and profit objectives achieved. This issue is further elaborated in the case study later in this chapter.

The next market question is "How much will people be willing to pay?" A common way to address this question is to determine what people pay for comparable products and services. This can be accomplished during the naturalist phase. You can also ask people directly about pricing of the product concepts that you show them during the marketing phase. Formal market studies may also prove useful.

The last market question is "How much revenue can we expect?" This is a difficult question because it requires that you forecast the time until market penetration and the likely growth of market share, perhaps of a market that is also growing in size. If you have a year or two of history with early versions of the product or service, such forecasts become easier. Many times you can use the life-cycle data for comparable products as a baseline.

The answers to these market questions describe the opportunity and the likely results of your taking advantage of this opportunity. These answers do not explain how you will pursue this opportunity and what competitive forces you will have to overcome to succeed. These issues are considered in the section of the strategic plan that describes the product offering being proposed.

I should note that many approaches to business planning characterize the competition in the discussion of the market opportunity. This is certainly reasonable. However, I find it more useful to consider the competition in the context of what you are proposing to do. The reason for this is elaborated as the product-related questions are considered.

The first product question is "What specific functionality will be provided?" To answer this question, you can employ the evolutionary architectures construct introduced in Chapter 3. You start with Level C—the vision—and formulate a concept delight the marketplace in terms of the answers to the questions just discussed. As emphasized when this constr introduced, the thinking underlying the Level C product vision should not be constrained by time, money, technology, and so forth. Your only goal is to define what will ultimately delight the marketplace.

From a business-planning point of view, this vision serves two important purposes. First, the nature of Level C drives the definition of Level A and then of Level B. In this way, an evolutionary product family is created.

Second, Level C describes where the market wants to go. If you cannot envision a path from your Level A to an *eventual* Level C, then the plan you are developing may be fundamentally flawed. This is due to the fact that what the markets wants will eventually be provided, if not by you then by someone else. Your inability to envision how you can ever provide what is wanted does not mean that other potential offerors will also be unable to respond. It is reasonable to assume that one or more competitors will respond, and then your product family will be in trouble.

This conclusion may cause you to abandon the plan in question. Alternatively, it may cause you to seek resources beyond those of your own enterprise. For example, you might hire consultants to gain the needed expertise. Alternatively, you might form a joint venture with another enterprise. Yet another alternative is to acquire or merge with an enterprise that has the requisite resources.

Once Level C is defined, the next step is defining Level A. The Level A member of your product family is the means for revenue, either now or in the near future. Thus, getting Level A into the marketplace should be, at most, an engineering, manufacturing, and marketing problem. If it is also an R&D problem, you should scale back on Level A to eliminate the unknowns for which R&D is needed.

Creation of Level B, on the other hand, may involve resolving a variety of R&D issues. The Level B member of the product family should provide substantial enhancements over the Level A product. These enhancements may be available in perhaps six months (for software products) or as much as three to five years. Thus, there tends to be some time for R&D efforts. The Level C vision also should affect the R&D agenda.

It is useful to establish target dates for reaching milestones for Levels A and B. A typical milestone for Level A might be stated in terms of initial market penetration or perhaps achievement of particular sales goals, for example, the number of units sold. A typical Level B milestone is the demonstration of a "proof-of-concept" prototype.

These target dates are important because they drive many other aspects of the business plan. For example, the Level A milestone date would strongly affect when manufacturing facilities must be available and when packaging issues must be resolved. The Level B milestone date would drive, for instance, R&D plans.

Once the evolutionary product family is defined, including the nature of milestones and target dates, you next address the question "How will this functionality provide the desired benefits?" Answering this question is seldom as straightforward as people suppose. The focus is on evidence that the market will perceive the planned functionality as providing the benefits that it desires.

In some cases, this is a technical question. For instance, the aircraft market may be looking for an aircraft wing design that reduces drag by 3 percent. You may have wind-tunnel data that conclusively shows that your new airfoil design reduces drag by 3.21 percent. Therefore, to answer this question you need only cite the technical report that documents these results.

Most situations, however, are not so straightforward. Typically, the market's likely perceptions involve a complex mapping from features of a product to perceived benefits. For example, suppose that the market wants a home-management software package that supports all the financial, maintenance, food preparation, and inventory activities in the home. They want to manage their bank account, pay their bills, schedule maintenance of their home and themselves as well as be reminded of these appointments, plan meal menus, and produce weekly shopping lists for the grocery store, hardware store, and so forth. They also want a package that is easy to learn to use and easy to use once learned.

Given any particular design for an evolutionary product family that would provide these benefits, it would be very difficult to prove in a purely technical manner that this design would be positively perceived by the market. The only way to find out would be to query potential customers and other stakeholders, perhaps beginning in the marketing phase of the product-planning and design process. The results of these queries and others would provide you with the basis for answering this question concerning evidence that the functionality of the product is perceived as anticipated.

Assuming that there is compelling evidence that the planned product family will be perceived positively, the next product-oriented question is "What are the competing approaches to providing these benefits?" In other words, how might others attempt to provide customers with the same delights that your product family will offer. Two types of answer are of importance.

First and most obvious, this question dictates that you understand the competition and the products they offer and claim provide the benefits that you hope to provide. What are these products? Who sells them? On what basis do they compete—price, quality, service, image, and so forth? How do customers view them? What market share do they have? Answers to all but the last question can often be obtained during the naturalist and marketing phases. The last question usually requires that you pursue additional sources such as databases and industry publications.

A second aspect of this question concerns competing approaches that are very different from what you are planning. For example, I often find that high-tech companies are fairly perceptive regarding how alternative technologies might be employed to provide similar benefits. However, they often ignore low-tech or no-tech approaches. They forget that people can simply forego their technology-based products and continue with more traditional manual methods.

A good example of this type of situation occurs in training and education. I have been involved with the development of computer-based systems for training and education for almost 20 years. Computers can do some wonderful things in terms of animation, simulation, inference, and so on. While traditional training and education methods are perhaps far less capable in these areas, they have the advantage of being much less expensive and being the incumbent way of doing things. In this way, they are very strong competitors.

In general, this question is concerned with considering all reasonable alternatives to what you are planning and developing an understanding of the likely basis of competition with these alternatives. This type of analysis is central to knowing where to position your product family amidst the various alternatives. This type of thinking is also crucial for providing a basis for answering the next product-oriented question "Why will the competition let us succeed?"

This is one of my favorites among all the business-planning questions discussed in this chapter. I like it because it implies that competitors have intentions—they do *not* want you to succeed. Further, if you do succeed in penetrating the market or gaining market share, they will react. They may cut prices, increase marketing and sales efforts, or accelerate introduction of new-product offerings.

This question, therefore, is premised on your gaining an understanding of likely competitors' reactions and having a plan for dealing with these reactions. In my experience, Level B in your evolutionary product family can be an important component of how you deal with competitors. Level B embodies your next product offering, subsequent to introducing Level A to the marketplace. Thus, to an extent, Level B is your planned "counterpunch."

As reasonable as this seems, I find that people tend to have difficulty thinking this way. Getting Level A into the market seems to be all-consuming. Every bit of energy is focused on hitting target dates and keeping on budget. When you make it, or at least come close, there is a big sigh of relief. It's out!

The next period of time is, unfortunately, likely to be one where your competition pays more attention to your product than you do. They try to find its weaknesses and shortcomings. They create materials that argue for their offerings in terms of a lack of these weaknesses and shortcomings. Assuming that the marketplace is smart—which I think is the best way to proceed—it is reasonable to expect that competitors will find something to exploit.

Once you discover the nature of their challenge, what do you do? Often, some type of defensive strategy is quickly thrown together. However, in my opinion, you are already too late. You should be your own product's worst critic. You should know, in advance if possible, its weaknesses and shortcomings and how you plan to deal with them in Level B. You should plan to introduce Level B soon after your competitors have analyzed Level A and introduced their challenge. In this way, you change the whole game and send competitors back to the drawing board.

This approach to dealing with competitors works especially well when you are employing the two principles of evolutionary design introduced in Chapter 3:

First Principle: The underlying conceptual architecture should be capable of supporting Levels A, B, and C.

Second Principle: *Intrigue* stakeholders with Level C, *market* them Level B, and *sell* them Level A.

If your customers understand that you are evolving the product family in a way that is supportive of their needs for upward compatibility and if they are intrigued by the shared vision of where the product family is headed, your competitors will have a hard time crashing the party.

The final product-related question is "What will be the total costs of competing?" This question relates to the costs of developing, manufacturing, marketing, selling, and servicing your product. Within the scope of this chapter, it is not possible to discuss cost-accounting methods and their implementation. However, it is important to consider the issue of cost.

I have found that it is often surprisingly difficult to determine the cost of developing and introducing a new product, particularly if this is done in the context of an enterprise that has other ongoing lines of business. The difficulty is one of cost attribution. While it may be easy to attribute costs of direct labor, for example, it can be much more difficult to determine reasonable attributions of indirect costs.

The ongoing elements of the enterprise may require indirect functions, for example, government audits and contract administration, that the new-product development effort does not require. How much of these types of indirect costs do you allocate to the product development "cost center"? One answer is "As little as possible."

On the short term, this answer makes great sense. In this way, you avoid burdening the fledgling development effort. On the longer term, however, this approach can be problematic because it can result in underestimating the costs that will have to be borne once the product in question is a full-fledged portion of the enterprise's activities. If this happens, you may end up quoting customers prices that are less than your eventual cost of delivery.

I do not have a magic way to avoid this problem. However, this possibility dictates that you pay very careful attention to costs for both the short term and the longer term. This, in turn, requires that you scrutinize all the activities associated with developing, introducing, and servicing the product. All in all, this issue should be addressed by focusing on your processes and understanding the nature and costs of the activities that contribute or will contribute to this product effort.

The next set of questions is concerned with the technology that will enable creation of the product described in your plan. The word "technology" is used here to denote the means underlying your planned product, systems, or service. This can include things that are not often thought of as technology; for example, educational means such as lectures and discussion groups. Thus, technology should be interpreted as "technique," not just "high tech."

The first technology-related question is "How will the product functionality be realized?" This question is particularly important when a product embodies a new concept. In this case, the answer should provide evidence of the feasibility of creating the functionality proposed for this product.

This evidence need not be a technical treatise. It can be a brief summary that references documents or other materials, prototypes for example, that provide the necessary evidence. These documents can be internal proprietary reports or published accounts of the efforts leading to the required technical evidence.

A related product-oriented question is "What competitive advantage do we have?" If the technology just described provides a competitive advantage, the answer to this question should outline the nature of this advantage and how it will be used. The answer to this question can also outline other advantages such as established marketing and distribution channels, important reference sales, and superior manufacturing capabilities. It is important to also note any competitive disadvantages and how these deficiencies will be overcome.

The technology section of the strategic business plan is the place where I summarize all unknowns by answering the question "What unknowns remain?" Several of these unknowns may be technology related, especially if the planned product involves a new product concept. It is also common for there to be market-related unknowns—for example, the true size of the market and the nature of the competition. For all types of unknowns, it is important that they be acknowledged and that a means of dealing with these unknowns be specified.

A related question is "What are the risks?" Answering this question concerns understanding what can go wrong, the consequence of such things happening, and how you can hedge against such possibilities. One of the biggest risks I encounter is people's tendency to assume that they are in a much better competitive position than they actually are. Perhaps they have conceptualized a new way of solving an important problem. It is often almost impossible for them to entertain the likelihood that someone else has already developed this idea or perhaps has a better idea. Further, in many enterprises it is socially unacceptable to raise this possibility.

Another common risk is underestimating, sometimes dramatically, the time and resources needed to translate an appealing concept into a market success. A successful proof-of-concept prototype, for example, is just a start. Full-scale design and development, as well as creation of the means to manufacture, package, and service a product are very time consuming and expensive. Development of marketing and distribution channels can also be slower and more expensive than you might expect.

A somewhat subtle risk relates to the execution of plans. Perhaps the greatest risk to good plans is that they do not get executed. This seems to be a greater risk than poor execution. Many people have told me of excellent plans that got shelved. This lack of action is not, from what I can tell, related to people's not buying into plans. It is apparently due to the intervention of everyday life. People get so busy fighting forest fires they forget to plant new trees.

This problem falls squarely in the court of top management. It's their job to assure that people resources are allocated appropriately. It's their job to assess the enterprise's overall situation and assure that the allocation of resources is compatible with the enterprise's hierarchy of goals and plans. From this perspective, the risk of a lack of execution can be restated as the risk of a lack of attention and focus on the part of top management.

Summarizing briefly, our strategic business plan is defined by the strategic hierarchy that starts with the enterprise's mission, partitions pursuit of this mission into product areas, and defines one or more plans within each area. Each of these plans includes six sections, the first three of which are titled: (1) market, (2) product, and (3) technology. Completion of each of these three sections involves your answering a structured set of questions.

The remaining three sections of each plan are titled: (4) manufacturing, (5) service, and (6) R&D. Creation of these sections is not based on answering a standard set of questions, because the meaning of these three issues depends very much on the context of the plans being prepared. Nevertheless, it is possible to discuss the general nature of these sections.

Subordinate goals for manufacturing—what has to be produced, when is it needed, and at what cost—are driven by product goals. These needs may dictate a plan for development of new manufacturing processes that can meet these goals. On the other hand, as illustrated in Chapter 2, it may be most effective to design products for manufacturability in the sense that product design should capitalize on available manufacturing processes and infrastructure. In either case, the viability of a product—the ability to provide desired benefits at acceptable prices—is highly dependent on the costs of manufacturing. For this reason, manufacturing subplans are integrated into the overall business plan.

Service goals are also subordinate to product goals. There are two types of relationships. First, many products require support services for engineering modifications, training, and maintenance. There should be a plan for how these services will be delivered, what they will cost, and how they will be priced. For example, they may be priced separately to maintain relatively low baseline prices. Another possibility is to bundle some services into the baseline package, which increases the price but may provide customers with less uncertainty about their overall outlays.

A second role of the service plan is to outline how customer relationships will be created and maintained. Some services may be provided up front for free or at a nominal price—for example, audits or assessments of needs—in order to establish opportunities for selling products. Another possibility is to provide services that may be only indirectly related to the products of interest, but that may nevertheless serve to create the relationships that will be necessary for product sales. In all of these cases, the service function also provides your personnel with experience in the domains where your products are used.

R&D goals should be driven by Level B product goals, as well as by elements of the Level C product vision. This means that R&D is "pulled" by the enterprise's intentions, rather than R&D trying to "push" itself onto the business agenda. The elements of R&D driven by Level B are likely to be fairly concrete research problems that need to be solved to achieve Level B milestones. In contrast, the elements of Level C that influence R&D are likely to be somewhat "blue sky" and may involve basic advances in science as well as more applied research.

People have often asked me if this view of the role of R&D is too constraining. Shouldn't R&D be footloose and fetter free? I have pursued an answer to this question by asking the same question of many researchers and research managers in industry and other enterprises. The answer is unequivocal. Typically people say, "We would like our R&D efforts to be driven by the corporation's long-term product visions, but that requires our top management to have a long-term vision of what we will be delighting the marketplace with in 10 years. We are unaware of such a vision and doubt that it exists." Thus, to a great extent, R&D ends up pushing because all too often nobody is pulling.

The issues addressed by the subordinate goals for manufacturing, service, and R&D frequently cut across many product plans. Therefore, at the leaf level, the strategic hierarchy usually has leaves and branches that relate to multiple limbs. Explicitly depicting such relationships is often the first step in fully taking advantage of these synergies which, at the very least, help to lessen costly duplications of efforts. Explicit links also help to foster communication which, in itself, can greatly increase organizational efficiency and effectiveness.

EVALUATING PLANS

Given a strategic business plan such as described in the foregoing discussions, the next step in planning involves evaluating your plan's likely success and using evaluation results as a basis for improving the plan. I find it useful to evaluate plans in terms of the two broad categories of attributes listed in Figure 5.4—enterprise market potential and enterprise technology potential. These two sets of attributes are concerned with the extent to which your plan represents a market opportunity for the enterprise and the extent to which your plan shows that the enterprise is prepared to take advantage of this opportunity.

Enterprise market potential can be characterized in terms of potential unit sales and potential revenue per unit, where revenue can be thought of as gross or net revenue as explained shortly. Each of these two measures can be further decomposed.

ENTERPRISE MARKET POTENTIAL

- Market size

- Market share

- Revenue per unit

- Level of competition

ENTERPRISE TECHNOLOGY POTENTIAL

- Customer technology orientation

- Alternatives to technology

- Enterprise technology know-how

- Enterprise domain know-how

Figure 5.4 Attributes for Evaluating Plans

Potential unit sales can be related to potential market size and potential market share. Larger market sizes and larger shares of markets lead to greater potential unit sales. This evaluation is fairly straightforward except perhaps for establishing, if necessary, aspiration levels for unit sales.

Potential revenue per unit can be related to potential unit price (or profit) and potential competition. If the potential unit price (or profit) is high or very high and the potential competition is minimal or nonexistent, these attractive prices or profits will be realized. However, as the level of competition increases, potential prices or profits will be compromised via discounts and/or increased marketing and sales costs.

Note that potential revenue per unit can be interpreted as either gross or net revenue. In situations where net profit, perhaps as a percentage of sales, is dictated by the marketplace—for example, when selling to the government—one may want to focus on increasing gross sales rather than on decreasing costs. In contrast, in many commercial markets, customers drive selling prices but not the cost of selling and cost of goods sold. In such cases, the measure of interest may be net revenue per unit since this is the measure over which one has potential control.

Potential competition can be interpreted in at least two ways. One way is simply the number of players in the game, ranging perhaps from none to few to some to many. Another interpretation can be based on the intensity of the competition. In some cases, people with whom I have worked have rated the potential competition as extreme, even though there were only two or three competitors, because the competition for the available market was quite fierce.

Thus, the four attributes used to assess market potential include market size, market share, revenue per unit, and level of competition. The way in which you combine these four attributes into an overall index of market potential is totally enterprise dependent. Each enterprise needs to formulate its own tradeoffs among these four attributes, based to a great extent on its past experience with different situations and understanding those conditions under which the enterprise is more likely to succeed.

Enterprise technology potential is a broader and more general concept than simply the extent to which the enterprise has the technology (e.g., hardware and software) necessary for success. In a broad sense, this construct relates to the enterprise's abilities to marshal the means necessary to achieve the market ends characterized in terms of enterprise market potential. It is quite possible that some of these means may be far from high tech. However, they will represent the set of techniques plus knowledge (i.e., technology) that will enable success.

I think of technology potential as being a composite of two other constructs: technology importance and technology position. Technology importance can be decomposed into the attributes of customer technology orientation and alternatives to technology. If customers are both oriented toward your means of delivering the desired benefits and have no other alternatives, technology importance is very high. In contrast, if customers are not particularly oriented toward your technology and there is a variety of alternatives available, then the importance of your technology is very low.

Enterprise technology position can be related to enterprise technology know-how and enterprise domain know-how. Technology know-how, as the name implies, relates to the enterprise's expertise in the techniques and knowledge that will enable providing the products, systems, and services being planned. Enterprises tend to rate themselves high along this dimension, although I have seen a few cases where a bit of introspection lowered these ratings. In one case, all the expertise was associated with one individual and the lack of "bench strength" caused the lowering of ratings.

Domain know-how concerns understanding the domain of use of the product, system, or service. This understanding includes issues such as how the domain approaches technology in general, what other technologies your product must be compatible with, purchasing practices, maintenance philosophies, and many other issues. My experience has been that enterprises entering new domains tend to underestimate the importance of domain know-how. The result can be that *potentially* innovative products are dismissed as irrelevant.

Summarizing, the four attributes associated with enterprise technology potential include customer technology orientation, alternatives to technology, technology know-how, and domain know-how. These attributes can be weighted in various ways to

yield an overall metric for technology potential
are completely situation and enterprise specif
specify how they should be weighted.

130

to

However, it is possible to suggest how the
ing plans in this way can be employed. The obvious ~~
evaluating a plan is to score as high as possible in terms of the
eight attributes just described, as well as the weightings among
these attributes. My experience is that few plans are assessed as
being maximally positive along all eight attributes. There are
always shortfalls and tradeoffs.

Such results can be used to identify ways of improving plans.
A variety of rules can be applied to determining the best way to
pursue improvements. Sample rules include:

- It is easier to change yourself than to attempt to change
  the characteristics of the marketplace.

- It is easier to change market niches than to attempt to
  change the characteristics of a particular market niche.

- It may be easier to join forces with the competition rather
  than attempt to eliminate them.

- It may be easier to initially focus on technology-oriented
  customers and use them as reference sales upon which you
  can expand the market addressed.

- It is easier to hire domain expertise than it is to create new
  technologies and proprietary products and services.

- Decreasing the market size addressed tends to increase the
  potential market share.

- Decreasing the price tends to increase both potential market size and potential market share.

There are many more rules of this type. Some of them are
specific to enterprises that sell products rather than systems or
services. Others are quite context specific. By elaborating the set
of rules that applies in your enterprise and markets, you can use
assessments relative to the eight attributes as a means for making important improvements of your plans or possibly completely
rethinking them.

My experience has been that evaluation in this way can lead fundamental changes of plans. In one case, a small electronics company used this approach and found that they had much more uncertainty about the nature of the market than they had realized. A company in the computer market concluded that they needed a joint venture to overcome deficiencies in domain know-how, despite the fact that they had recently rejected a joint-venture proposal. A company in the engineering services market realized that they were in a much more competitive market than they had thought and considered how they could partner with other players in this market.

ORGANIZATIONAL IMPLICATIONS

One of the frequent questions I am asked about the planning process elaborated in this chapter concerns the organizational implications of this approach to strategic business planning. Put simply, people often ask, "Where is the organization chart in the hierarchy of mission, product areas, product plans, and so on?" A somewhat simplistic answer is "There isn't any!"

We can think about the hierarchy of plans as the set of hikes that the enterprise is pursuing or intending to pursue. Each of these hikes involves a cross-functional team that has devised the hiking plan and will take the hike—make it happen. Everyone in the enterprise should be involved in one or more hikes. The overall set of hikes should be mutually consistent and supportive. For example, experiences gained in one hike should pay off in terms of improvements in the plans for other hikes.

The overall set of hikes reflects the changes—the innovations—that the enterprise is pursuing. These changes should be continual and, I would argue, should be viewed as the most important activities of your enterprise. From this point of view, it seems quite reasonable to claim that the hierarchy of plans *is* the organization. Your role in the enterprise is to contribute to formulating goals and plans and then to executing plans and achieving goals. The fact that your background is in marketing, engineering, or finance influences the skills that you bring to the game, but not the nature of the game.

I realize that this is a bit too simple. There still needs some matrixing whereby all the marketing types, engin finance people, and so forth, have a "home." However, they should not spend much time there—they need to be on hikes. Further, the organizational chart that depicts the hierarchical relationships between functional areas should be as flat as possible and not play a central role in the activities of the enterprise.

What does this imply for top management? Basically, I think that the members of the top management team should think of themselves as planners and leaders of hikes. They should facilitate the formation of hiking teams. They should coach team members in how to plan hikes. They should go on quite a few hikes, not at the front but back in the pack helping people deal with long inclines and other frustrations. They should epitomize the concept of collaboration rather than control.

To succeed in this role, top managers have to become adept at understanding their hikers. This includes understanding people's abilities, limitations, inclinations, and preferences. Such understanding provides the basis for configuring hiking teams and choosing hikes so that teams continually gain skills and experiences that are central to the enterprise's future.

CASE STUDY

The remainder of this chapter is devoted to a case study. This case study focuses on development of the strategic business plan associated with the software tools discussed in Chapter 3. In this way, we can see how product plans become central elements of strategic business plans.

As noted in Chapter 3, this case study is based on experience with my own company. The choice of this case study was influenced by the need to have intimate knowledge of the development of the strategic plan discussed, as well as the discretion to relate the plan in this book. The goal in discussing this case study is to provide you with insights into developing a strategic plan rather than to argue the merits of this specific plan.

This business area emerged from our traditional business in intelligent software systems for supporting operators, maintainers, and designers of complex systems such as aircraft and power plants. As noted in Chapter 3, it started with a workshop on human-centered product planning and design, and evolved to include a workshop on strategic business planning and, fairly recently, a workshop on understanding and facilitating organizational change.

These workshops, as well as subsequent software tools and consulting services, were driven by customers' requests and by referrals from satisfied customers. After a year or so, we began to see the possibilities for these products and services to become a strong business area. This realization led to the creation of a business plan using the methodology described in this chapter.

The first step was to define the mission of the enterprise. It seemed natural to begin with Search Technology's mission statement:

> To provide customers with innovative products, tools, and services that tangibly support and enhance human interaction with complex systems.

Adoption of the company's broad mission statement was reasonable, but after a year or so it began to feel much too general. This feeling eventually led to a more specific statement:

> To provide customers with innovative products, tools, and services that tangibly support and enhance their abilities to plan and design new products and services, develop and execute strategic business plans, and understand and manage the organizational changes necessary to accomplish these ends.

With a mission statement formulated, the next step was to define product areas. The initial business plan defined three areas: seminars, software tools, and training simulators. The seminars—later repackaged as workshops—and the software tools were described in Chapter 3. The training simulators are computer-based organizational simulations that enable trainees to experience virtual organizations. We had built two of these simulators for customers, and the business plan reflected aspirations to create off-the-shelf versions of these types of training devices.

Representing the enterprise in terms of these three product areas seemed quite reasonable—after all, these three types of products and services were what we were selling. However, after a year or so of representing ourselves in this way, we came to realize that these product areas did not make sense from a market-oriented perspective. Customers did not inherently want seminars or software. They had problems they wanted help in solving.

Consequently, the business plan was substantially reorganized and revised to include three product areas: new-product-planning, strategic business planning, and organizational change planning. Within each of these areas, three products plans were defined: one for workshops, one for software tools, and one for consulting services. Simulators became an advanced approach to the training provided by the workshops. This representation focuses squarely on the problems that customers want help in solving, as well as on the methods and tools for helping them.

Thus, this strategic business plan included three product areas with three product plans in each area, yielding a total of nine product plans. While these product plans differed in important ways, it would be much too cumbersome to discuss each of the nine plans in this chapter. Instead, the discussion focuses on each of the primary sections of these plans (i.e., market, product, and technology) and considers the overall nature of the answers to the key questions outlined earlier in this chapter and summarized in Figure 5.3.

What benefits will the product or service provide? Note that this first market-related question is also the first concern in the product planning and design methodology. The nature of the benefits sought by the marketplace is a key link between product and business planning. In product planning, we assure that the desired benefits are embodied in the product or service. In business planning, we formulate the means for getting these benefits into customers' hands at competitive prices that yield an acceptable profit.

The benefits provided by the products and services described in these nine plans are, in general, the same—good plans quickly. More specifically, these products and services provide the means for efficiently formulating plans that you can execute with confidence. The objects of these plans are new products, the overall nature of the enterprise, or organizational change.

Who wants these benefits? An obvious answer is the top management of most enterprises. However, as noted in Chapter 3, top management, in my experience, spends surprisingly little time planning new products, business strategies, and organizational changes. While top management may prompt planning initiatives and review results, the people charged with planning are usually heads of the planning function or the finance function. Heads of units of 50 to perhaps 500 people within much larger enterprises also often lead planning efforts.

How many people want these benefits? Initially, we thought of this market in terms of the 250,000 technology-oriented companies in the United States. This market seemed appropriate because of the technology-based nature of our methods and tools. Further, we felt that our understanding of a range of technologies would give us an advantage in terms of domain knowledge.

We soon learned, however, that not all of these companies are planning oriented. Further, unless they were facing major changes, they often saw no need to plan. They focused solely on trying to get better and better at doing what they had always done.

We came to realize that we needed to focus on companies that are compelled to change. When the future is expected to be very much like the past, planning efforts can be minimal. In contrast, when enterprises see substantial and inevitable changes staring them in the face, planning becomes a priority. This realization led us to focus on enterprises facing the following types of changes:

- Competing in global rather than just domestic markets

- Converting from defense to commercial markets

- Dealing with downsizing of corporate functions

- Adopting "lean" methods of manufacturing

- Shifting from mainframe to distributed computing

- Becoming constituency oriented rather than institution oriented

There are a large number of enterprises in such situations. While it was very difficult to estimate the number of such enterprises, it became clear that selling planning products and services to these types of enterprises would be much easier than selling to technology-based enterprises in general. While the market size might be smaller, the probability of success for any particular sale would be much higher.

How will the product or service be purchased? Our first approach was to use our existing customer base and referrals from these customers as the sole means for identifying potential customers for planning products and services. This worked well for a year or so.

To expand we needed additional mechanisms. A mix of methods was adopted. We made contacts through trade associations by, for example, getting onto the dinner-speaking circuit. Industry consortia also proved to be mechanisms whereby we could gain access to a sizable number of companies.

Another channel was created by joining forces with a few of our very large competitors, namely large consulting firms. They supported our selling of our planning products and services as a means to, in effect, fill out their range of offerings. Not surprisingly, the customers they brought to us in this way proved to be very open to our types of solution.

Yet another mechanism, especially for smaller companies, was referrals via these companies' lawyers, bankers, accountants, insurance agents, and peers. Top management in smaller companies are often also the owners. When faced with problems or opportunities where planning might help, these managers/owners typically rely on their key advisors, who include the types of people just noted.

Thus, the business plan included four channels through which to market and distribute our planning products and services: our own customer network, trade associations and industry consortia, large consulting firms, and referrals from professionals supporting small businesses. Leads identified in this way were followed up by direct selling, initially via telephone and subsequently in person.

How much will people be willing to pay for these benefits? When this business plan was represented in terms of seminars or workshops and software tools, the answer to this question concerned how much people were willing to pay for these products and services. This assumes that they want these products and services.

However, as noted earlier, people are much less interested in these things than they are in having their problems solved. Workshops and software tools may be the means, but they are not what people are buying. They are buying solutions. Thus, the "how much" question has to be recast. How much are people willing to pay for substantive help in planning new products, formulating business strategies, and dealing with organizational changes?

My experience has been that our customers have paid at least $100,000 to $150,000 to "name brand" consulting firms for assistance with the types of problems we are discussing. We have been able to sell competitive services for $30,000 to $50,000 and provide software tools as part of the overall package. Numerous customers have told me that our prices are a bargain.

Turning now to the product-related questions: *What specific functionality will be provided by the product or service?* The answer to this question was considered in detail in Chapter 3. The evolutionary product family with Levels A, B, and C is a primary link between product planning and strategic business planning. In fact, in the software tools for these two areas, there is a link that enables exporting these elements of a product plan directly into elements of the corresponding business plan.

How will this functionality provide the desired benefits? This question can usually be answered using the results of the naturalist and marketing phases discussed in Chapter 3. Hence, the answer for this case study of business planning is provided in the discussion of product planning in Chapter 3. This illustrates yet another link between the two methodologies.

What are the competing approaches to providing these benefits? There are many, many consulting companies that provide services to assist customers with the types of problems targeted by this business plan. There are also a few software tools available, although none as yet that are as comprehensive. Thus, there are numerous real competitors in this market.

An equally important competitor is the status quo. Our concepts, principles, methods, and tools for planning challenge many customers' ways of thinking about their enterprise, the marketplace, and so on. While we find that many potential customers find these new ways of thinking very compelling, they are nonetheless apprehensive about changing their ways. In many cases, the status quo wins the competition for this reason.

Why will competition let us succeed? A primary advantage that we have is our focus on empowering customers to solve their own problems. Our workshops and software tools are intended to train and aid people to deal with their own planning problems. In contrast, the vast majority of the competitors in this arena hope to sell customers their consulting services for as long as possible.

Somewhat ironically, as indicated in Chapter 3, we have added consulting services to our overall package to give customers confidence that their problems will be solved. However, we emphasize our goal of empowering them and then leaving. In other words, as a few customers have told us, we help them to wean themselves from our assistance as soon as is reasonable.

This does not imply that we no longer do business with them. However, this business is in new areas and may involve new methodologies. By not forcing customers to depend on us, we find they often choose to depend on us more. My guess is that they do not worry about us taking them captive.

Considering the technology-related questions, the first question is *how will the product functionality be realized?* This question can be answered on at least two levels. On a concrete level, the answer for the software tools is Visual C++ running on Microsoft Windows. This is very straightforward and needs no elaboration.

On a more abstract level, our technology is the methodologies that underlie the workshops and tools. We have conducted extensive research to gain an understanding of how to develop methodologies that are easy to learn to use, as well as easy to use. We have learned how to package these methodologies in ways that enable creation of good plans quickly. Put simply, the ways in which we have formulated planning problems are much more innovative than the software language and environment that we chose to use to embody these formulations.

What competitive advantage do we have? The best answer to this question is the one that our customers give. We have a comprehensive and integrated set of concepts, principles, methods, and tools for dealing with the interrelated problems of planning new products, business strategies, and organizational change. These offerings are supported by training, via workshops and simulators, that enhances people's potential to perform, as well as aiding, via software tools and consulting services, that directly augments performance. Our customers have said that they have found no comparable offerings.

IMPLEMENTING PLANS

The foregoing discussion has briefly provided the flavor of a strategic business plan developed using the methodology presented in this chapter. The plan discussed in this case study has evolved substantially since it was first formulated. As noted earlier, the representation of this business area has changed as we have come to better understand the nature of this market. Further, our strategies have evolved as we have experimented with different marketing and distribution channels. I expect this plan will continue to evolve. The lessons learned in executing the first year of each five-year plan will lead to a substantially revised five-year plan the following year.

This may seem odd. We only get to execute one year of a five-year plan before we rethink the plan. Why don't we maintain our commitment to the original plan? Wasn't it a good plan? It was good at the time it was prepared and that enabled us to execute it with confidence. However, we learn a lot by executing our plans. We learn enough to know that the original plan is not as good as we thought. So we revise the plan.

Succinctly, planning enables execution. Execution enables learning. Learning enables planning. This cycle leads to continual change and growth. In this way, we find innovative means to pursue of our mission.

SUMMARY

The strategic business-planning methodology introduced in this chapter is fairly straightforward. You begin by defining the mission of the enterprise from the perspective of the marketplace by answering the who, where, what, and how questions. You then define the strategic hierarchy in terms of product areas and product plans, again from the perspective of the marketplace.

Two types of difficulties can slow progress for these first two steps of the process. One difficulty concerns adopting the perspective of the marketplace. The natural tendency is to view the world with a self-centered orientation. Thus, for example, I frequently find that enterprises characterize benefits from the point of view of the seller not the buyer. Fortunately, the skill needed to be able to see things from the market's point of view is a skill that is readily learnable.

The other difficulty concerns reaching consensus. By consensus, I do not mean that everyone agrees on every element of the strategic plan—disagreement is inevitable and healthy. Instead, consensus means that everyone agrees to commit themselves to executing the plan to the best of their abilities, despite any underlying disagreement about the market opportunity and appropriate strategies and tactics. Team-oriented planning can help to build consensus. However, sometimes what is most needed is maturity, which is difficult to gain quickly.

Each plan within the strategic hierarchy includes six sections: market, product, technology, manufacturing, service, and R&D. There are standard questions within each section, although I find that as groups gain experience with this methodology, they tend to modify, add, or delete questions. In effect, they create their own methodology using the elements of planning presented in this chapter as a starting point.

Plans can be evaluated and improved using a hierarchy of eight market-oriented and technology-oriented attributes. In other words, evaluation involves using eight attributes that characterize the nature of the opportunity and the ability of the enterprise to pursue this opportunity. Market potential is assessed in terms of potential market share, market size, unit prices, and competition. Technology potential is assessed in terms of customer technology orientation, alternatives to technology, enterprise technology know-how, and enterprise domain know-how.

I have found that this hierarchy, displayed graphically, provides an excellent vehicle for groups to use collaboratively in critiquing plans, as well as in finding creative ways to improve plans. The structure of the hierarchy forces the group to focus. The analysis rules, examples of which were discussed earlier, prompt the group to think along particular attributes, which often leads to creative interpretations and significant improvements.

This approach to planning has important implications for the enterprise's organizational chart. By focusing on what the enterprise is trying to accomplish rather than on the functions whereby it gets accomplished, you can substantially lessen the chances of institutionalization. In an institution, people strive to become a director or vice president of one function or another. Turf gets created and defended, even when it is no longer relevant.

If the enterprise instead focuses on the strategic hierarchy, people focus on gaining responsibilities for the enterprise's key plans. They know where the enterprise is headed, and they want a turn in the driver's seat. While functional areas may exist to support these efforts, there is no inherent reason for them to exist beyond the support they provide to pursuing the plans in the strategic hierarchy.

The case study discussed in this chapter, in conjunction with the case study discussed in Chapter 3, provides a glimpse into how product planning and design relate to strategic business planning. These two case studies also show how a few central concepts persist throughout the planning process.

For example, by focusing on stakeholders and their perceptions of viability, acceptability, and validity during the product-planning process, you can very easily deal with the benefits questions, as well as the evidence that your products provide these benefits, during the business-planning process. Another instance of the integration of the two processes relates to the evolutionary architectures construct. The notion of Levels A, B, and C is pervasive within these methodologies.

My experience is that these approaches to planning appeal to a wide range of enterprise types. They provide a means of alleviating the fundamental difficulties of planning: not knowing what to do, taking a long time to do it, and not creating anything of value. Nevertheless, many enterprises encounter problems in implementing these methodologies.

These problems are often due to conflicts between the belief systems underlying their old way of doing things and the belief systems they must create if they are to successfully adopt these human-centered, market-oriented approaches. The organizational team is accustomed to taking certain kinds of hikes. They have unconsciously created a set of beliefs about the nature of the marketplace, expectations of customers, roles of technology, the value of innovation, and so on.

Faced with the need to change fundamentally, they usually quickly see that these methodologies provide quite reasonable ways to proceed. However, the new types of hikes envisioned often require different skills and types of teams. The existing team, unfortunately, assumes that they can succeed at new hikes without changing themselves. As a result, success does not come as quickly as hoped, if at all.

This problem is exacerbated if the enterprise has to maintain the old belief system while also creating the new one. If part of the business still focuses on traditional markets (e.g., defense contracts) while the other part emphasizes new markets (e.g., commercial products), it is quite likely that confusion will result. The old belief system will be threatened and become fragmented while the new belief system will be burdened by the baggage of the old system.

While methods for diagnosing and dealing with these types of problems are discussed in Chapter 7, it is useful to consider briefly how these problems are affected by use of the strategic planning methodology presented in this chapter.

First, as noted earlier, the strategic hierarchy and its constituent plans clearly portray the portfolio of hikes the enterprise is pursuing. For instance, differences in the ways the market-related questions are answered for different plans should enable understanding the ways in which the enterprise has to address the various markets it is pursuing.

Second, the team-oriented approach to planning tends to substantially increase communication. With appropriate leadership, especially in the areas of values and culture, the ways in which elements of traditional belief systems need to be differentiated or interwoven with elements of new belief systems can be continually refined. Leadership in this context does not necessarily mean being at the head of all the hikers. More important is dropping back and hiking with stragglers to help them understand what to expect and how to deal with frustrations.

One of the primary frustrations is likely to be associated with the fact that you are not taking the types of hikes you used to take. Hard-earned hiking skills may no longer be central to the enterprise's success. In such situations, leadership involves communicating the needs for change, the roles that will result, and the skills necessary to fill these roles.

Thus, leading change involves focusing on external stakeholders to assure that the right types of changes are chosen and on internal stakeholders to help people to commit to these changes and contribute to their success. From this perspective, human-centered design can provide you with the means of creating the type of enterprise that can successfully implement human-centered design for its products, systems, and services.

One type of stakeholder has yet to receive much attention in this book—you. As a member of top management in a small, medium, or large enterprise in the public or private sector, you are a key stakeholder. What does this imply for your product planning or business planning?

One answer is that you should lead and epitomize the enterprise's total commitment to delighting customers. You should continually communicate and demonstrate this commitment. This answer is a good one, but totally inadequate.

The ultimate answer concerns why you are in the business of running this enterprise. What are your short-term and long-term personal goals and plans? How is being a leader of this enterprise compatible with these personal aspirations?

Many people find these questions rather overwhelming. Others often approach these questions in an almost trivial way. We do not like to be challenged to make our lives consistent and integrated. While we would like to view ourselves as authentic, we usually are not sure how to achieve this somewhat amorphous end. In Chapters 6 and 7, we focus on discovering answers to these types of questions.

6

Discovery

*Discovery is a process whereby you
and the world uncover and create your
story and your part in larger and longer stories.*

As with earlier chapters on product planning and business planning, this chapter approaches the problem of life planning—including, for example, personal aspirations, expectations, and choices—by first considering a metaphor that will help in dealing with these issues. This metaphor is discovery which, in this chapter, is concerned with uncovering and understanding other cultures and societies.

This type of discovery can yield many insights that provide a basis for other types of discovery. The external discovery of the world can provide the means, as well as the impetus, for the internal discovery of yourself. This chapter deals with the external. The next chapter addresses the internal.

Discovery provides a metaphor that is useful for life planning because discovery involves planning a process but not its results. Ventures, or adventures, to discover other societies and cultures can be planned, but the discoveries themselves can seldom be planned. Life planning can be a similar process.

Before elaborating the nature of discovery and its relationships with life planning, it is useful to ask some very basic questions. Why worry about it at all? Why not just let life happen? Isn't that about all you can do anyway?

Perhaps predictably, the attitudes underlying these types or questions often produce behaviors that are dysfunctional relative to the pursuit of innovative products, businesses, and lives. These attitudes reflect an outlook captured in Thoreau's well-known statement, "The masses of men lead lives of quiet desperation." To the extent that this is true, innovation is undermined.

I often encounter groups of top and middle managers where attitude problems are their primary difficulties. They believe, for example, that markets are unfair, governments are incompetent, and corporate parents are unreasonable. Were it not for these factors, they believe that they would be tremendously successful. Unfortunately, they feel that they are relatively helpless in the face of these external forces.

My involvement with such groups is usually related to helping them create plans for some type of new direction in their enterprise. First, however, I often have to uncover and portray the group's beliefs about issues such as just noted. Then, I have to get them to realize that these beliefs and attitudes represent their most fundamental barrier to success.

I do not think that such situations are inevitable. Individuals and organizations do not inherently have to become inbred and rigid. They can learn how to recognize and accept situations needing change, as well as learn how to discover better trails to hike.

DISCOVERY AS A PROCESS

Discovery can be viewed as a process that involves several steps or phases. The first step involves forming intentions and deciding to explore and pursue adventure. This sounds simpler than it usually is. Often you need a plan—at least a plane ticket—and resources to enable the pursuit of your adventure.

More difficult, however, is the commitment to the types of change that may result from discovery. If you head off to explore, for example, other cultures in developing countries, there is a very good chance you will be strongly affected by your experiences. This is particularly true if you pursue this exploration in the true spirit of discovery, as elaborated in this chapter.

people see this possibility as a risk. They are not sure
ant to entertain change, especially if the nature of this
uncertain. I think that this is due in part to their not
being sure of who they are now. They are not sure of themselves
and do not know how they will deal with change. I return to this
issue in Chapter 7.

With intentions formed, the next step involves placing yourself in situations that allow or perhaps even enable opportunities
for discovery. Since you cannot fully know what discoveries may
occur, I like to think of this step in terms of placing yourself in the
path of serendipity or, better yet, at the crossroads of serendipity.
By placing yourself in situations where change is endemic, you
know that something will happen. Serendipity is involved in that
whatever happens will affect you.

I have felt this sense that things are happening in rural
Bolivian villages, on the dusty roads in South African homelands,
in the old city of Jerusalem on Palm Sunday, at the border
between East and West Germany on the night the border ended,
and in St. Petersburg during the short-lived coup. There is a
heightened sense of reality and often a feeling that I am observing
myself as part of this reality.

This type of feeling is most likely if you pursue the next step
of discovery, namely, immersing yourself in the environment you
are exploring. This usually requires that you let go of the safety
net that most of us carry through life. By getting involved and
making commitments, we accept, at least implicitly, the risks
associated with the environment. You cease being a tourist and, if
only temporarily, become an immigrant.

I often have this experience with the many enterprises that I
help with planning. For a few days or weeks, I completely
immerse myself in their problems and opportunities. I become
committed to helping to make sure that particular things happen.
I begin to see what it means to be part of this enterprise's culture.

Throughout this process of placing and immersing yourself in
environments you wish to explore, a central task is observing and
listening. This involves asking questions, paying careful attention
to answers, and sharing relevant experiences and feelings. This

task is essential if you are to gain an understanding of stakeholders and how they view their world.

The final step of discovery—at least the final step within a particular period of discovery—concerns reflecting and interpreting. This involves noting connections and distinctions. Connections are links among observations and constructs, for example needs and beliefs, inferred from these observations. Connections provide a means for clustering observations and reducing the complexity of the data.

Distinctions, in contrast, enable elaboration of the complexities of the data. In this type of analysis, you attempt to distinguish different kinds of constructs and relationships that affect behaviors in the environment of interest. For example, you might identify sequential or hierarchical relationships among constructs that appear to govern the likely courses of events.

To illustrate, in Chapter 7 the needs-beliefs-perceptions model is discussed. This simple model characterizes relationships between people's needs and beliefs as they affect their perceptions and decisions. In collecting information with which to elaborate this model, I accumulated a substantial quantity of books, papers, and reports that included results related to needs, beliefs, and perceptions.

Analyses of this information led me to conclude that many types of needs and beliefs could be clustered—that is, they could be connected. However, there were several distinctions among clusters that seemed to be essential, particularly in terms of potential relationships among clusters. Thus, the process of identifying connections and distinctions was essential to elaborating this model.

A central question in the process of discovery is "What is the world like?" To answer this question fully, you must consider, contrast, and experience what is versus what might be. The status quo can be overwhelming. Consequently, it requires substantial effort to delve below the surface and understand the possibilities of what might be versus the often compelling reality of what is.

This process can be viewed as one of creating an evolving world model that embodies connections and distinctions across markets, societies, and cultures. From this perspective, discovery is a process of continually modifying and extending your world model by placing and immersing yourself in different environments, observing and listening while in these environments, and reflecting and interpreting relative to the experiences gained and data collected.

DECIDING WHERE TO EXPLORE

Pursuit of the steps or phases of discovery depends on being able to answer the very basic question "Where to explore?" Most of us answer this question implicitly. We first venture outside our hometowns. This may initially be with our parents or relatives, but eventually we go alone or with peers.

I grew up in a small New England seacoast town with a population, at that time, of about 6,000. My first adventure of discovery as a teenager was going to Boston with my girlfriend in my 1949 Chevy that I had bought for $35. It was wonderful and a bit scary. In fact, I still find driving in Boston a little scary.

In Boston, we discovered universities, museums, swan boats, and Chinese food. We discovered several places where members of both sides of our family had lived many years before. Put simply, we began to see ourselves in a larger context. Later, we moved to Boston for graduate school and, for several years, this city became the center of our universe with, for example, trips to Florida being our adventures.

Most of us go through this process of broadening our horizons. We come to see the peculiarities of our roots. Many of these peculiarities we embrace. Some we reject. Many stay near their roots. Many move on.

The next level of exploration often expands beyond one's country. For me and for many other people, this exploration focuses on understanding Western culture. These roots lead to Europe. I have had the good fortune of being in a profession that has taken me to Europe many times, once to live in The Netherlands for a year.

The "standard tour" of Western culture starts in Greece, moves to Italy, and then proceeds to France, England, Germany, and so on, depending on the nature of your roots or interests. In these countries, you can steep yourself in art, history, and architecture. You can visit the birthplaces of famous writers, painters, and composers. Basically, you can take a living course in "Western Civ." that was often so boring in college.

At first this course is wonderful. After repeated experiences, for me at least, it became a bit tedious. I became much more interested in the Europe of today. This Europe cannot be found in cathedrals and museums. You have to frequent pubs, clubs, markets, the workplace, and local churches. Later, I consider what you do while you are in such places.

There is a tendency to think that once we are familiar with Western culture, we have broadened ourselves sufficiently. However, for me, the East has always beckoned. This leads to an interesting question. Where is the East?

A colleague once asked me, "Isn't it odd that we think of the roots of Western culture as coming from the Middle East? What has 'middle' got to do with the Middle East?" My guess it that "middle" refers to an area that is in the middle between West and East.

Nevertheless, the East starts for me along a line running through St. Petersburg in Russia, Istanbul in Turkey, and Jerusalem in Israel. In these cities, I have felt and seen things that are not European, juxtaposed with other things that are very much European. If my history is correct, the European aspects of these cities arrived much more recently than Eastern influences.

Moving east, my nearest experience is India. While you can feel the effects of British occupation, India is clearly of the East. My other experiences are in Japan and Taiwan where you can see much that has a Western flavor, but you would never mistakenly conclude that you are in the West. I suppose that the East ends in Hawaii, where Western influences start to dominate.

Perhaps the most striking differences between East and West are associated with philosophies and religions. The monotheistic religions of the West—Judaism, Christianity, and Islam—encourage world views that are quite different from those of Hinduism, Buddhism, Taoism, and Confucianism. Succinctly and much too simply, the difference is between a personal God and an impersonal cosmic order. A variety of other differences is discussed later in this chapter, as well as in Chapter 7.

Most of the types of exploration discussed thus far have focused on the developed world, or the developed portions of the countries mentioned. Another level of exploration involves developing countries or developing sectors of countries. Parts of Greece, Spain, and Turkey, in my experience, are in this category. Major parts of India and South Africa, as well as the whole of Bolivia and Zimbabwe, are in the developing category. There are, of course, many others. I have limited my examples to countries where I have direct experience of the developing nature of their economies and societies.

In these places, the effects of economics and education are overwhelmingly obvious. You meet people whose primary goal in life is to eat tonight. You deal with people whose many medical afflictions could be alleviated at the corner drug store in the developed countries. You also can feel a very basic, uncomplicated sense of family and place. In churches, you can experience the wonder of hundreds of a cappella voices singing familiar hymns, often in unfamiliar languages, and feel your spine tingle at the power of the music.

Another avenue of exploration involves crossing sectors of society. I have held university faculty positions in the United States and Europe. I have been involved in business transactions in many countries, in both the East and West. I have provided advice and consultation for the United States government and for those of several other countries. There are many connections and distinctions among academia, business, and government, in the United States and internationally.

As an example, I have found that the defense industry worldwide is fairly homogenous compared to, for instance, differences between defense and commercial industries within countries. In other words, defense contractors are much more alike, regardless of country, than are a defense company and a commercial company within any given country. As a consequence, virtually all defense companies are pursuing similar strategies, at least in part, for dealing with declining defense markets—they are inundating developing countries with low-priced offers for weapon systems.

There are many types of answers to the question "Where to explore?" For the most part, they all involve broadening your horizons which, of course, depends on the current scope of your horizon. Therefore, I cannot suggest which answer is best for you. However, it is possible to suggest how you should pursue discoveries in whatever environment you choose to explore.

DECIDING HOW TO EXPLORE

My approach to exploration draws upon the human-centered design methodology discussed in Chapter 3. The first step involves identifying stakeholders and determining their concerns, values, and perceptions. This step can be pursued at several levels.

For example, earlier I noted that many people travel to Europe seeking Western civilization. From an historical and geographical perspective, this involves gaining first-hand knowledge of the emergence of the various countries in Europe and how their maturation was affected by, for instance, the Renaissance, Reformation, French Revolution, and Industrial Revolution. This knowledge might be gained by visiting numerous historical buildings, monuments, and battlefields.

Another point of view is socioeconomic and political. This involves learning about the evolution of social and economic issues and their influences on forms of government, as well as on expectations of the public and private sectors. This knowledge might be pursued by studying the nature and origins of literature, art, and music, as well as by visiting birthplaces of the more influential contributors in these areas.

Yet another perspective is local and contemporary. Knowledge of this type could be gained by visiting with people in cities and villages. Working for a period in a country is a way of learning numerous details of how people manage their daily lives. One of our favorite tactics when staying with friends in another country has been to ask them to spend the day—often Saturday or Sunday—exactly the way they would spend it if we were not there. This has resulted in numerous low-key afternoons in parks feeding fish and ducks, or in pubs chatting about soccer or upcoming elections.

Ideally, exploration involves gaining and integrating knowledge from all of these perspectives. A bit of homework can provide a good start. Reading history books, historical novels, and contemporary fiction can be very helpful. Newspaper articles are particularly useful for providing an overview of current events and issues.

The goal of this background work, as well as of the actual exploration in the field, is to identify stakeholders and relationships among stakeholders, including the reasons that such relationships emerged. Understanding these stakeholders involves determining the needs, beliefs, and desires that drive their behaviors. Chapter 7 describes a methodology for pursuing this understanding.

While background reading can provide a good start, the naturalist phase of exploration involves immersion in the environment of interest. In my experience, naturalist activities are best pursued in other than museums, cathedrals, palaces, and castles. In such places you are likely to meet the family from Savannah who is pleased to meet someone from Atlanta and suggests that everyone have lunch together. This is not the way to explore.

Another venue of little use is the bars and restaurants in business hotels. While you may be in Africa or South America, this is where you meet the salesman from California who wants to chat about the upcoming series between the San Francisco Giants and the Atlanta Braves. I can enjoy such discussions, but not while I am exploring.

My favorite places for immersion are local pubs and clubs such as found in England, Ireland, Germany, and The Netherlands. Sidewalk cafes in France, Italy, Spain, and Greece provide similar opportunities. Gardens and parks in England, The Netherlands, and Japan enable mingling with the locals. Neighborhood churches in Bolivia and South Africa have allowed glimpses into local lives. When we were living in The Netherlands, many days spent walking the seacoast provided a sense of how the Dutch and many others escaped and relaxed.

The universal meeting place is the market or grocery store. I often spend many hours perusing the variety of offerings in crowded, noisy, and aromatic markets. The surroundings are often shabby at best, and occasionally elegant, but everyone shares the same goals when they are there. They select from among the bounty and then discuss, haggle, argue, and so on until they depart with brimming bags for the evening meal or perhaps a weekend feast.

Meals are a good place to get people talking about concerns, values, and perceptions. Wine or beer helps but is not necessary. The sharing of food, in itself, seems conducive to the sharing of oneself. My naturalizing often makes great progress over lingering meals where economics, politics, religions,—virtually everything—are fair game.

In this process, you discover stakeholders and their needs, beliefs, perceptions, and desires. You also usually gain an appreciation for their competencies and resources. Their competencies include the knowledge and skills with which they deal with the world. Resources include natural, social, cultural, political, and economic means of accomplishing things.

People's behaviors are greatly affected by the resources available, and they develop competencies that take advantage of these resources. Geography and climate affect what people eat and wear. They also affect people's metaphors and world view in general.

For example, I am struck by the apparent effect of climate on attitudes. In areas where there are long periods without much sun—for example, England, The Netherlands, and Seattle—I have found that people seem more dour, perhaps even depressed, during these periods. I can recall reading several scientific studies that support this conclusion.

Consciously or unconsciously, people adapt to their environments. They learn to employ available resources and develop competencies that enable them to satisfy their needs and desires. While these resources and competencies may be very different from yours, this does not mean that these people are particularly different. They have simply adapted to their environment as you have to yours.

Your world model should take this phenomenon into account. The similarities within our species are more striking than the differences. In fact, I would argue that the similarities within the animal world are more notable than the differences. Yet, our perceptual and psychological wiring has prepared us to focus on differences, often judging the worth of humans by differences that are merely adaptations to, or the results of, differing environments.

Below the surface of perceptions and behaviors, there are aspirations and expectations. There are also needs and beliefs. For discovery to serve as a useful metaphor for life planning, you must delve below this surface. You need to explore the basis for other people's behaviors as a precursor to exploring below your own surface.

All people appear to aspire to material well-being. However, the concept of well being varies significantly across contexts. In most of the world, aspirations focus on food, housing, and education, as well as on relationships within families and society. In developed countries, however, we tend to take the basics for granted and aspire to self-actualization. This seems to be particularly true in the West.

My experience in developing countries is that aspirations are very concrete. It is very clear what people want, and they are often struggling to satisfy basic needs and help their children avoid their footsteps by, for example, obtaining an education. Most, if not all, of this struggle they bear on their own shoulders. They know that they have to act.

People's aspirations in developed countries are more complicated. I have encountered many people in their mid to late thirties, often with Ph.D. degrees, who are not yet sure what they will do in life. They have tried a few different types of jobs, perhaps in academia, industry, and government, and found them all lacking. They have often also tried a variety of relationships with the same conclusion.

Such people tend to be in search of the self-actualization that they were raised to believe is the only appropriate quest. However, they are not sure what self-actualization means to them. They do not have a vision, calling, or fire in the belly. They have made it through all the wickets that society has laid out, and now they are lost. They are often disillusioned and dispirited.

Another frequent experience has occurred in pubs in England and Ireland in particular. I have met many people who are in marginal or dead-end jobs, or perhaps unemployed. They are barely meeting basic needs and see absolutely no prospects of things getting better. Their aspirations may no longer include a home or flat of their own and may not even include children.

A related situation is associated with strong trends toward delayering, downsizing, and right-sizing in developed countries. These terms all mean that companies are eliminating massive numbers of jobs. Even for those companies that are still very profitable, it is now socially acceptable and perhaps expected that companies regularly thin their ranks.

I have read that recently dismissed middle managers in the United States often suffer from two types of malaise. One is the type of depression usually associated with being fired or laid off. There is a mixture of guilt and anger with which people have to deal.

The second, and relatively new, type of depression concerns the recognition that your type of white-collar job is disappearing. Not only have you lost your job, but also you will never get a similar job again. People who earned college degrees and did everything else society demanded of them have never experienced this type of dead end before.

Aspirations, as well as the lack of aspirations, are integral to life planning, which is discussed in Chapter 7. Another key element is expectations. In fact, aspirations and expectations tend to interact. Often people aspire to things that they expect can happen and avoid aspirations for things that they do not expect can happen.

Expectations seem to vary across contexts. In much of the world, struggling to meet basic needs is expected and success is hoped for, but not necessarily expected. Nevertheless, people aspire to meet these needs because they have no other choice. Ennui will not feed the family. In such situations, when success occurs, it often prompts a celebration.

In the developed world, we have tended to expect the best in jobs, housing, mates, and sports teams. Many people in our society have taken most of these things for granted. Recently, however,

:tations have not been fulfilled. For example, a college s no longer a guaranteed ticket to an ever-increasing f living. A job with a Fortune 500 company no longer provides guaranteed security. There are fewer and fewer guarantees in general.

The combination of aspirations and expectations tends to strongly influence the overall attitudes with which people approach the world. People who are clawing their way up the lower rungs of the economic ladder often exhibit an amazing level of optimism, at least from the point of view of an outside observer. In contrast, people making very sluggish progress, if any, on the higher rungs of the ladder often seem burdened with self-doubt and anger. Your world model would be woefully inadequate if such effects of aspirations and expectations were ignored.

When asking people about their aspirations and expectations, I am often struck by how much people are stuck in the here and now. Often their aspirations are quite modest and their expectations low. This seems to be prevalent in lower and middle classes in *developed* countries.

One of the types of evidence upon which I base this conclusion is a large number of long naturalist conversations in bars, pubs, and sidewalk cafes in a variety of countries. There is a high level of cynicism with regard to government, big business, the military, the church, and so on. I imagine that this type of cynicism has always existed. What is more problematic, however, is the sense that things will not and cannot get better.

Another type of evidence comes from an informal survey that I conducted about one year ago. I asked roughly 30 people the following question: "What percentage of people, aged 35 to 45, would you say feel that life has not worked out as they had hoped—they are not necessarily sure of what they hoped, but they are clearly disappointed?" The answers ranged from 60 percent to 90 percent, with the dominant tendency toward the high end.

I have no way of knowing if these estimates are correct, or even close to the actual percentage. Nevertheless, what might they mean? It seems to me that many people have had a rather generic sense of the "good life" that they felt they could expect. Their aspirations have been similarly vague and ambiguous.

Whatever they have achieved does not feel as good as they thought it would feel.

In contrast, in *developing* countries I have been very impressed with people's grand visions, particularly for their children. In taking very little for granted, they are forced to act to feed their families, educate their children, and secure better jobs. They simply cannot accept being stuck in the here and now.

A concrete example of this tendency is the aggressive, entrepreneurial streaks in the street vendors and taxi drivers that I frequently encounter in developing countries. Another example is the extent to which all family members work to improve the family's standard of living. Members of the family or the village need each other if they are all to survive and achieve some level of prosperity.

Much of this apparent attitude difference between developed and developing countries may be due to geography, climate, urban versus rural settings, and relative economic trends. Nevertheless, this difference is very interesting. My guess is that a key element of this difference concerns the reluctance to change within developed countries and the overwhelming desire for change in developing countries.

I wonder, however, if this distinction may diminish as the developed world increasingly accepts change as inherently more natural than the lack of change. There never were that many guarantees. We just thought there were. If change is accepted as inherent, perhaps aspirations and expectations, approached meaningfully, can again be central to personal transformation and growth. This possibility is pursued in Chapters 7 and 8.

Summarizing the discussion thus far in this chapter, discovery is a multistep process that involves identifying stakeholders and determining their concerns, values, and perceptions, as well as their underlying needs and beliefs. This includes understanding resources, competencies, aspirations, expectations, and attitudes. An important element of this understanding involves seeing connections and distinctions across cultures and economic classes.

STORIES

The metaphor of discovery provides a means for gaining insights into yourself, as well as into your society and culture. By looking through the glasses of other societies and cultures, you are able to see yourself as part of larger wholes. You can see your story as part of larger and longer stories.

To illustrate, my frequent business dealings in a wide variety of countries lead me to conclude that American beliefs, values, business practices, and so forth, reflect physical, psychological, and social needs common to all humankind. We all seek food, clothing, and shelter for ourselves and our families. We all want to belong. We all want to invest ourselves in meaningful activities. We all want to maintain self-esteem.

Of course, the things to which we attach meaning and the ways in which we achieve self-esteem can vary significantly among cultures. Thus, our beliefs, values, and so on, are also particular to the set of experiences that has nurtured our culture. In the United States, for example, we attach great value to being individuals, owning guns, and creating lists of the Top Ten of virtually everything in life. In my experience, these penchants are seldom encountered elsewhere.

How did this orientation arise? My guess is that it's due to the fact that the United States still had a frontier less than one hundred years ago. Further, the people who chose to immigrate to this frontier country were among the more independent of the population from whence they came. Finally, the Western cultural roots of European immigrants tend to be more individually oriented than other cultures.

The notion that we have much in common with all humankind, but are also shaped by our environment and our experiences, can be applied to understanding other countries and areas. For instance, my experiences in troubled areas such as South Africa and the Middle East have led me to find much in common with businesspeople and families in these areas. However, their concerns, perceptions, and values are also shaped by many years of strife, fear, and anger.

I cannot help but wonder if Americans' reputation for being very open and trusting does not reflect our relative isolation from the seemingly endless stresses experienced in these troubled areas. Imagining myself in such environments quickly leads me to conclude that I also could easily develop a "wolf is at the door" mentality. In this way, experiences in such areas provide very strong glasses with which to view your own society and culture.

You can also learn much from experiences that cut across economic class boundaries, as well as across cultural boundaries. A few years ago, I spent a week or so in Bolivia on the altiplano working with a medical team visiting dusty villages with mud houses and a wide variety of health-related problems. I was fascinated by the children with whom I could converse a bit in my halting Spanish.

What struck me most was their eyes. After a few days, I began to feel that I was seeing myself looking at me, smiling, laughing, and sometimes crying. I began to be able to imagine myself in their situation. I felt a strong need to seize the day, not so much in Bolivia but in my own life back in the United States.

More recently, I have spent some time in Bophuthatswana, one of the "homelands" created by South Africa to which many blacks were forced to migrate. I spent one afternoon walking in a small town, talking with students from a high school where a friend of mine is chaplain. The students were very curious about why an American would visit them. I joked about my being there to make sure that my friend was doing a good job.

The students became sufficiently comfortable to lapse into everyday discussions about problems, especially boy-girl problems and arguments about music. At one point, one of the students tried to explain their dilemma to me by saying it was just like a recent episode of the TV show "Knots' Landing". I was forced to admit that I had never seen this show, although I was aware it existed.

The students were very surprised. They were also very pleased that they could explain something about the United States to me! They were 8,000 miles farther away from Hollywood than me, but they had in some ways better knowledge than I had. While I was surprised that they even had televisions—often powered by small gas generators—they were surprised that I would avoid such wonderful entertainment. My world model concerning how African teenagers spend their time required some serious modifications. I imagine their model of Americans was revised a bit also.

These types of experiences also provide very strong glasses with which to view your own society and culture. Poor, struggling Bolivians can lift your spirits and South Africans, who are also struggling but not in the same way, can educate you about your own country. This is the way discovery happens.

The rewards likely to result from these kinds of exploration are heavily influenced by the perspective from which the exploration is taken. An important dichotomy concerns your orientation toward the world—a simple distinction is that of exclusivity versus inclusivity. An exclusive perspective emphasizes we versus they—it focuses on differences. In contrast, inclusion implies a widening circle, within which you see your life, and that of your society and culture, integrated with more and more of humanity and nature—the emphasis is on similarities.

In a sense, inclusivity can be viewed as "we are all in the same boat." I experienced this sense in another trip to South Africa. A friend invited me to go to a church meeting with him. As we rode to Bloemfontein to go to the meeting, I was looking forward to experiencing several hundred a cappella voices singing familiar hymns.

We went into the church and sat near the back. Within a few minutes, a well-dressed man approached my friend and asked to be introduced to me. Once the introduction was complete, he asked me to leave. Actually, he started by saying that he was sure I was a wonderful and honorable person. However, I could not stay.

The reason, of course, was totally obvious. I was the only white in a group of several hundred blacks. I did not belong. I wanted to be there, but they did not want me to be there. I was discriminated against!

Ironically, it struck me that this was an experience of inclusivity. I was able to feel a bit of the discrimination they had felt all their lives. Of course, I really could not sense the full impact of discrimination. Being white, self-confident, and reasonably well off economically dramatically limits my ability to feel the oppression they have felt.

Inclusivity does not, however, mean that we all are alike and experience things in the same ways. Instead, it means that we are committed to being open to others' perceptions and experiences. It means that we accept and embrace others. In the process, we discover the many things we have in common and come to understand our relatively few differences.

An important aspect of this discovery process involves understanding and creating stories. Each of us is involved in an unfolding story, both personally and in a larger and longer sense. To discover yourself, you need to understand your current story and how it will or might unfold.

Such discovery can be enabled by reflecting on the central stories of other societies and cultures. This can be done in several ways. As noted earlier, reading history and historical fiction can provide tremendous insights into how a particular culture emerged and has evolved.

The myths and legends that are central to a culture can be learned in this way. As Joseph Campbell has illustrated in *The Power of Myth* and other works, many myths are common across cultures. For example, many cultures have stories of saviors who are born of virgins, die, and are resurrected. Most of humankind apparently has needs for such a story.

Contemporary fiction can also provide insights. This is also true of music, art, dance, and so on. I am particularly fascinated by the music of developing countries. For instance, I find the music of Bolivia to be haunting, as is the country. The protest music of South Africa brings me back to the protest movement of my college days.

The stories that I find most interesting are what might be called "street stories." These are the stories told by the proverbial man (or woman) in the street. These stories are not about mythical or legendary characters. They are about everyday people and common events, crises, and celebrations in their lives. Growing up. Adventures that were not supposed to happen. Failures and successes of marriages, families, businesses, and relationships in general. The rich uncle. The famous uncle. The black sheep in the family.

I have heard these types of stories over and over again in many contexts ranging from the dusty, dilapidated villages in developing countries to the fashionable upscale salons in many of the world's most glamorous cities. The details of such stories matter little. What really matters is the commonality of these stories across all people. We all share many physical, psychological, and social needs. We all experience similar joys, passions, disappointments, and frustrations. We all have relationships with many people who love us, hurt us, and share our victories and defeats. Put simply, we are all connected.

Stories are more pervasive than we might expect. Much of our communication, much of our sharing of knowledge, happens via stories. A simple example is the way in which many people share their vacation experiences. When they come back to the office after having been on vacation, they might just provide their colleagues with, in effect, a list of their experiences and what they learned. However, they do not do this. Instead, they tell the story of their vacation, often many times for many different listeners.

They are not just imparting facts. They are sharing experiences. They are sharing themselves, in part because they like attention and admiration, and in part because such sharing is an element of the social system in which they participate.

This phenomenon extends far beyond vacations. When the software engineers in my company discuss how to address various software problems, they often resort to stories of past projects where similar issues were faced. They relate vignettes of successes and failures.

There are also many marketing and sales stories, contract negotiation stories, and personal stories about picnics, Christmas parties, and adventures in the marketplace. All of these stories have immediate, practical value. At least as important, however, is the role they serve in communicating and perpetuating our company's culture. This mechanism helps us when we are integrating new people into our culture and hurts us when we are trying to make essential changes. Stories persist, despite best laid plans to pursue different hikes.

Discovery of people's stories can lead to many insights. By focusing on the similarities among all of our stories, you can see the many powerful themes that are common across all humankind. This not only helps you to feel inclusively connected to all people. It helps you to make sense of your own situation and proceed more creatively and productively.

RELATIONSHIPS

As noted in many of the discussions in earlier chapters, relationships are central. This is true for discovery as well as for woodworking and hiking. In this chapter, I have focused on relationships with your group and society, as well as with all humankind. An important element of discovery involves recognizing the roles that relationships play in general, as well as the roles they play in your life.

To a great extent, the essence of discovery is relationships. Exploration of any culture or society involves gaining an understanding of people's individual relationships with each other, their broader relationships in their community, and their relationships with their environment. A particularly interesting aspect of such relationships concerns the relative roles of the individual and the community.

In the United States, individual rights are paramount. Rights such as free speech, owning a gun, and not mowing your lawn are all cherished elements of our culture. In contrast to our extreme individualism, many cultures are more communitarian. Understanding and accepting your role in the community, as well as respecting elders, are examples of how cultures such as the Chinese and Japanese differ from the United States.

Explorations of these and other cultures can provide insights into our relatively self-centered, accomplishment-oriented society. For example, you could reasonably argue that our fascination with Eastern cultures has influenced our thinking about family, community, and the environment. Similar fascination with native American cultures has also influenced our thinking on these issues. These are examples of discovery at work.

While relationships can be the objects of discovery, they also can be the means to discovery. Relationships with wood, tools, trails, equipment, and people can provide the avenue for discovering them and yourself. Dialogues with these animate and inanimate "partners" can be central.

A large portion of such dialogues often involves sharing personal stories. Much of the time is spent listening, asking questions, and responding to questions. For example, my aforementioned interactions with the Bolivian children involved their asking me about where I came from and what it is like and my asking them about the village, their school, the songs they were singing. In this process, I learned about the Bolivians' yearning to regain the land, particularly the seacoast, they had lost to Peru in a war many years ago. This emerged from asking the children about the enchanting song they were singing.

In the earlier discussions of relationships, the distinction between control and collaboration was noted. Most of us have an inbred tendency to try to control the process of discovery. We try to organize the process, be intentional about relationships, and make sure that we are learning as much as we think we should.

On the surface, this inclination seems reasonable, perhaps even laudable. However, this degree of control can get in the way of discovery. While you can place yourself in the likely path of serendipity, you cannot and should not attempt to control what comes down the path. Instead, you should try to collaborate with the course of events. This means that you take things as they come. You remain open to what might be discovered.

Often, nothing seems to be discovered. Familiar patterns repeat, and exploration seems almost routine. After a while, however, connections and distinctions among various scraps of experience come together and you begin to see novelty in the routine. The stage is then set for transformation and growth as discussed in Chapter 8.

Collaboration is a theme throughout this book. My experience is that you can calmly deal with frustrations and setbacks in woodworking, hiking, and discovery by not expecting to be in control, but by aspiring to collaboration. Working together provides the means for moving forward or, if necessary, embarking on trails that are somewhat different or substantially different.

Beyond serving as a metaphor for life planning, discovery also provides passions all its own. The emotional side of discovery is rich with sights, sounds, smells, joys, and disappointments. This richness adds much to the adventure.

One of my favorite collections of sights, sounds, and smells is bazaars. In Bombay, Istanbul, Kyoto, La Paz, and Taipei, to name a few, I have been fascinated by the vastness of what humans and the rest of nature can produce. The numbers of kinds of foods, trinkets, pets, and practical things seem unlimited. The varieties of sales pitches and approaches to haggling, as well as the experiences of bargaining victories and defeats, provide a wonderful backdrop for discovery.

I am also fascinated by the numbers of people who have gone before us and built alcazars in Spain, forums in Rome, temples in Greece, and walls in Jerusalem. The succession of victories and defeats, winners and losers, monuments and ruins, and so on, are captured for me by a phrase used by a colleague who was guiding me around the old city of Jerusalem.

He was showing me various ruins and stages of history of the city as displayed by the types of stones and construction methods underlying existing buildings. I commented on the fact that so many conquerors and rulers had come and gone in the city's long history. He said that the "teeth of time" inevitably led to their passing. Discovery often involves following the tracks of these teeth of time and coming to understand the ebb and flow of relationships.

In contrast, nature often seems more timeless, or at least we have more difficulty sensing the tectonic movements of nature. An example of this sense of timelessness occurred for me in Zimbabwe in Hwange National Park, a large game preserve. We had traveled for roughly four hours from our hotel at Victoria Falls on the Zambezie River. Our guide stopped on a hill overlooking a large watering hole. He brought out plates, wine glasses, and an elegant lunch that we ate perched on this hill as we watched zebra, wart hogs, and many other animals come to get water. It struck me that, except for us and our glasses of wine, this scene may have been repeated almost every day for thousands of years.

Another aspect of passion is music. I have mentioned some of the more compelling examples earlier in this chapter. The haunting music of Bolivia. The powerful a cappella church performances in Africa. The organ music in European cathedrals and the ballads in Irish pubs are elements of the passion of music.

Not all examples of the emotion of discovery are joyous. Working with a medical team in Bolivia provided many sad moments. I can vividly recall the sadness and helplessness of a peasant child upon being told that her disease was incurable and she would never grow up. In a culture where her primary role was to give birth and raise children, she would never have any. The emotions of such situations, both in your eyes and theirs, provide the indelible ink of discovery.

DISCOVERY AS A METAPHOR

Discovery can be pursued in many contexts. Woodworking, hiking, traveling, doing business, and helping others with their enterprises have all provided me with venues for discovery. I have heard many stories, and also told quite a few. Such experiences can help you to see how your small story fits into a much larger and longer context. It can help you to understand the roles that you play in these larger and longer stories.

Planning the process of discovery involves immersing yourself in the unfamiliar and letting go so as to open yourself to discovering the unanticipated. This requires that you explore the uncharted—at least not charted in your experience. In this exploration, you may encounter the path of serendipity or, better yet, the crossroads of serendipity.

From this perspective, discovery provides an excellent metaphor for life planning. For the most part, you cannot design and determine your life in any exact fashion. All you can do is plan a process of education and experiences that will give you the potential to pursue your vision, mission, or calling.

We are ready to change our point of view from external to internal, from the outside world to the inside world. Life planning is also a process of discovery. The object of that discovery is you and your abilities, limitations, inclinations, and preferences.

To consider life planning, the issues raised in this chapter are recast into a much more personal framework. Chapter 7 discusses and illustrates this framework. Chapter 8 shows how this framework, as well as the material discussed in earlier chapters, can provide the basis for personal transformation and growth.

7

Life
Planning

*Needs and beliefs affect what knowledge
is gained, what facts are sought,
and how both are interpreted.*

Life planning? Many people have suggested that this phrase is an oxymoron. They claim that the words "life" and "planning" do not make sense together in the same phrase. These people argue that, despite our best intentions, life just happens. We have much less *control* than we think we have.

However, perhaps control is not what you need. Maybe the key is *collaboration*, as it was for product and business planning? This collaboration involves understanding yourself and your relationships with family, community, environment, and so on. Seeking this understanding is a process of discovery.

NATURE VERSUS NURTURE

The process of discovering yourself, and creating or adjusting your life plans accordingly, involves understanding the components of yourself that are due to "nature" and "nurture." Understanding your true nature can enable you to understand how to be comfortable with yourself. This involves understanding needs, beliefs, abilities, aptitudes, and inclinations.

Understanding these components of your nature can be particularly important when what you are doing is not "natural."

Consequently, you may be working much harder, investing more energy, and having much less fun than others. While there is nothing wrong with working hard and expending energy, it certainly is desirable for the demands of your tasks to match your abilities and inclinations.

It never ceases to amaze me how much time people say they spend doing things they claim not to value. At the same time, they emphasize how little time they spend doing things they profess *to* value. People often tend to reflect wistfully on all the things they wish they were doing. However, they do not act. In this way, they squander their time. They are wasting their most precious resource.

The other side of nature is nurture. Understanding how you have been nurtured frees you to entertain different perspectives, lifestyles, values, and so on, without feeling that you are rejecting something absolute or something that is the essence of yourself. You can gain an understanding of the extent to which your beliefs, values, and so on, are mainly products of the time and place where you were born and raised. In this way, you can embrace other cultures without losing your identity.

Unfortunately, people often find other cultures threatening. Belief systems and values, as well as food and clothing, that are different from theirs are often suspect. I think that a primary basis for this suspicion is people's general lack of understanding of the true nature of their own belief systems, values, and so on. Consequently, they are afraid of the challenge that other systems potentially present.

The internal discovery of your nature and how you have been nurtured provides the foundation upon which life plans can be built. It can be argued that this discovery process operates on two levels, at least. On one level, you discover how to discover. This was the topic of Chapter 6. Then, on another level, you actually discover who you are, what your society and culture reflects and values, and how integration and authenticity might be achieved. This is the topic of this chapter.

NEEDS, BELIEFS, AND PERCEPTIONS

I often have the opportunity to talk with people about their personal goals. Many of these people are in their twenties and thirties. They are trying to find a vision, mission, or calling. Others are in their forties or fifties. They are trying to reorient their lives, perhaps because their current "hikes" are no longer appealing or, in many cases, have been eliminated in corporate downsizing.

The process of choosing goals and fully committing yourself to pursuing them is often very difficult. In my experience, people's perceptions of the world tend to get in the way of this process. People jump too quickly to focusing on *their perceptions* of the opportunities available, as well as on *their perceptions* of the demands that their families and communities place upon them.

I think that the focus on perceptions, as well as flawed perceptions, are primary reasons that people have such difficulty choosing personal goals and planning accordingly. To move beyond this apparent barrier, you need to consider the nature of perceptions and how they arise.

One view is that perceptions are formed by the interaction of your accumulated knowledge and the information at hand, that is, the stated facts. While this seems reasonable, it is a totally inadequate explanation for the purposes of this chapter. You need to get below the surface of perceptions.

Extensive study of this topic has led me to a much deeper explanation. I have concluded that people's knowledge and the stated facts are not the sole determinants of perceptions. People's needs and beliefs affect what knowledge is gained, what facts are sought, and how both are interpreted.

Thus, deep understanding of perceptions requires that you understand the needs and beliefs that influence perceptions. Before pursuing this deeper understanding, it is important to consider what you can do with this understanding once you have it. How will understanding your needs and beliefs help you in life planning?

A simple answer is that your life plans should satisfy your needs and be compatible with your beliefs. This answer is much too simple in that once you understand your beliefs, you are likely to embark on a course to change some of them. Further, many beliefs are adopted, in effect, to satisfy needs. Therefore, the ways in which needs are met may have to be reexamined to enable the transformation and growth you seek.

The notion that people have needs was popularized by Abraham Maslow in the 1950s. He argued that people have a hierarchy of needs including:

- Physiological

- Safety

- Belongingness and love

- Esteem

- Self-actualization

Maslow's theory was that people would always satisfy lower-level needs such as safety, before pursing satisfaction of higher-level needs such as self-actualization. While there is little evidence to support this hierarchical relationship, the notion of five distinct classes of needs has persisted.

These five types of needs can be termed situational needs in that changing situations, for example, drought and famine, can affect what needs are predominant. Another class of needs is termed dispositional in that these needs are inherent in particular individuals. David McCelland is among the foremost investigators of these types of needs. He has studied four types:

- Achievement

- Power

- Affiliation

- Avoidance

Of particular interest, he has considered the likely behaviors of individuals with various mixes of these characteristics.

The results of his research indicate that people with a high need to achieve tend to be those who are strongly oriented toward improving task performance and accepting personal responsibility for performance. They also tend to have a great desire for performance feedback. People with these characteristics make good entrepreneurs.

The need for power was found to represent a concern for impacting people and things. The power motive leads to openly competitive and assertive behavior, particularly among men. People with high needs for power, coupled with a high degree of internal inhibition (i.e., control of impulses), tend to assume positions of leadership in voluntary organizations and believe in centralized authority, hard work, self-sacrifice, and charity. They make good managers in business enterprises, especially if their need for affiliation is low.

People with a high need for affiliation tend to perform better when opportunities to relate to other people are present. Such people invest in maintaining personal networks. They emphasize cooperation, conformity, and avoidance of conflict. Because of desires to be liked by everyone, they tend to perform poorly as managers.

McClelland has also studied a variety of avoidance motives, including fears of failure, rejection, success, and power. Fear of failure—which I have encountered in several employees who were hired because of their perfect or near-perfect college records—has been found to be associated with the parenting practices with which one was raised. Fear of rejection has been found to be associated with fear of failure and a high need for affiliation. Fear of success tends to be higher for women who fear social rejection based on performance success. Fear of power is associated with concerns that one's assertiveness will lead to rejection by others.

The situational and dispositional needs studied by Maslow and McClelland, respectively, can be elaborated if a particular context is chosen. I have studied the domains of culture and religion, science and technology, and business enterprises. For each of these domains, it was possible to derive a long list of context-specific needs that could be roughly organized using Maslow's and McClelland's categories.

Industrial/organizational psychologists have particular instruments—questionnaires and interview protocols—that they can use to assess the extent to which an individual has the types of needs just discussed. They also have other instruments for assessing other aspects of people's psychological orientations—for example, the Myers-Briggs personality types. They use the results of such assessments to provide career counseling and other kinds of advice. In the absence of such results, it is difficult to reach specific conclusions about how your needs should affect your life planning. It is possible, however, to consider a few general conclusions.

For instance, in the technology-based enterprises with whom I frequently work, I have found that achievement needs lead technical people to excel, the reward for which is promotion to management. Unfortunately, many of these people appear to lack the power needs associated with success in management. They also seem to often have moderate to high needs for affiliation, which undermines their success as managers. The result tends to be a well-liked, technically oriented failure as a manager.

I also find quite a few people who are very risk adverse, which, I think, reflects avoidance needs. Fear of failure—in terms of not being technically correct—as well as fears of rejection appear to lead people to hide in very narrow areas of expertise. The only way I have found to deal with this is to either reconceptualize the notion of failure or change beliefs about the likelihood of failure. In both cases, you must consider the nature of beliefs.

Beliefs are those things that are held to be true, that is, consistent with fact or reality. The phenomena of belief involves a wide range of life, including belief that the Earth orbits the Sun, belief that a low-fat diet is good for you, belief that freedom is a right of all humans, and belief in a power greater than humankind. Notice that beliefs are *held* to be true, not necessarily *proven* to be true. Thus, seldom can you prove someone's beliefs to be wrong. Occasionally, you can convince someone that their beliefs are dysfunctional.

Three aspects of beliefs are of interest in this chapter. One aspect concerns beliefs or expectations of what will happen. Another aspect is beliefs or explanations of why something has happened. Third are beliefs about how things work—for example, the mechanisms underlying organizational processes.

Expectancy theory provides a model of the role of beliefs in decision making. This theory asserts that the perceived relative attractiveness of various options is related to people's beliefs about the consequences to which each option will lead, as well as to their beliefs about the desirability of these consequences. In situations where consequences and/or desirability is uncertain, the theory includes subjective probabilities to discount these risks.

From a life-planning perspective, expectancy theory can provide a basis for exploring your options. For each option, if you choose to pursue it, what consequences do you believe are likely? How desirable are these consequences? What uncertainties do you have in answering these questions?

Most people can think of all the great things that might happen if they pursue a particular path, and they can imagine how desirable these consequences would be. With multiple options, people might be in a position of weighing alternative paths to greatness. However, in my experience, this seldom occurs.

There are two reasons. First, given people's needs for achievement, power, and affiliation, as well as their inherent interests, there usually are not very many alternatives, at least not many are entertained. Second, people often focus on undesirable consequences as well as on desirable consequences.

When considering an option, people realize that both good and bad consequences could result. I could start a business and become rich, or I might fail and end up bankrupt. I could try to become president of my division and end up in charge, or I might fall short and have to play second fiddle for a long time.

I have talked with many, many people about these types of decisions. As noted in Chapter 6, quite often people assert that they do not want to aspire to anything they do not expect will occur. They say that they do not want to be disappointed. They do not want to fail.

Many people seem to associate failure with not achieving specified targets. If you aspire to be number one in the widget market, but succeed only in becoming number two, you have failed. If you aspire to double sales and only increase sales by 80 percent, you have failed. I completely disagree with this outlook.

There are very few failures in life. There are likely to be very many setbacks, but few failures. Based on this philosophy, I focus on desirable consequences. Patiently and persistently, I try to make these consequences happen. If they do not occur—and it is seldom an all-or-none situation—I try to use what I learn from such setbacks as the basis for trying again, perhaps with a somewhat modified goal. While I attempt to ascertain possible negative consequences, I devote little energy to worrying about them.

Another aspect of beliefs concerns people's explanations for why particular consequences occur. Attribution theory provides insights into the causal relationships that people attribute to results they observe. This theory, or collection of theories, is concerned with people's inferences with regard to causation, as well as the consequences of these inferences.

Studies of people's attributions typically focus on inferences about the causes of people's behaviors. Attributions, once assessed, are usually categorized in terms of the nature of the causes attributed to observed behaviors. One category concerns situational versus dispositional causes. If observed behaviors are believed to be dictated by characteristics of the situation (e.g., an employer may have no choice but to let an employee go), then the attributed cause is termed situational. In contrast, if observed behaviors are believed to be due to personal characteristics of the observed person (e.g., an employer may let an employee go because he or she does not like the worker), then the attributed cause is called dispositional.

A related category of attributions is external versus internal. This category concerns whether behaviors are caused by external forces or internal motivations. For instance, a salesman's excellent sales performance might be attributed to his luck in being assigned to a region where sales are easy (an external cause) or to his superior sales ability (an internal cause). Similarly, good performance might be attributed to chance (an external cause) or to skill (an internal cause).

One of the most important and interesting findings of research in attribution theory has been what is termed the fundamental attribution error—the tendency to overestimate dispositional causes of behavior. In other words, observed behaviors are often due more to the nature of the situation than to the characteristics of the actor. Nevertheless, observers tend to attribute causation to the actor's disposition. Thus, for example, negative perceptions of potential organizational changes or resolutions of disputes over strategies often run afoul of incorrect attributions of intentions. People may attribute decisions to insensitivity of management, for instance, when, in fact, the nature of situations may dictate particular changes or resolutions.

When people are asked to attribute cause to the results of their own behaviors, their attribution errors are somewhat different. They tend to attribute positive results to dispositional causes and negative results to situational causes. When things go well, it's due to their strong abilities and great efforts. When things go poorly, it's due to impossible assignments, inept customers, or bad luck.

I have seen these phenomena many times, both in my company and in the companies that I help with planning. Fundamental internal problems are often externalized. The market is inscrutable. The government is inept. Corporate parents are unfair. Once these explanations become predominant, the organization tends to become helpless. People spend much of their time talking about the many external causes of their problems and little time trying to solve the real internal problems.

This can also happen to individuals and become a potentially insurmountable barrier to life planning. Most people seem reluctant to focus on the internal causes of their current situation in life. They attribute their previous decisions and commitments, many of which may have led to undesirable consequences, to situational characteristics dictating their choices. They may feel trapped by these consequences, and they may take solace that it is not "their fault" that they are in such a situation.

I advocate that you always assume internal causes for failures and external causes for successes. If you assume that you or your organization is the likely cause of undesirable consequences, then you can do something about it. If the customer is unhappy, then *you* have to do something about it. Similarly, if you are unhappy, then *you* have to do something about it.

On the other hand, if things go well, attribute your success to great customers, helpful suppliers, and hard-working employees. The more credit you share, the less likely you are to get too self-satisfied. Further, customers, suppliers, and employees will be ready and eager to work with you again.

It is also useful to attribute your personal successes to external causes. This will help you to pay attention to external factors. Further, it will help you to avoid becoming too self-confident. Most endeavors require other people, and you are more likely to succeed if you understand your needs for help.

I hasten to add that the position I am advocating should not be taken to extremes. If you pathologically accept blame for everything and credit for nothing, then self-esteem will wither. Nevertheless, on the average, I find that people have the opposite problem—their attributions are consistent with the aforementioned research findings

Attribution theory focuses on people's beliefs about other people's behaviors, intentions, values, priorities, and so on. This is just one class of beliefs. There is a wide range of phenomena about which people adopt or form beliefs, including nature, technology, organizations, and society.

The phrase "mental models" is often invoked to characterize people's understanding of the way the world works, or the way it might work. This construct has been adopted in many disciplines including psychology, management, architecture, and engineering. Reviewing these many uses of the phrase led to the following definition: Mental models are the mechanisms whereby humans are able to generate descriptions of why something exists and its form, explanations of its functioning and what it is doing, and predictions of what it is likely to do in the future.

The notion of a mental model can often be used to explain people's behaviors when these behaviors are other than as expected. For example, I noted earlier that I work quite frequently with cross-functional planning teams in a variety of enterprises. Cross-disciplinary skirmishes often occur with such groups.

A typical instance might occur when the marketing function advocates strategy X while the manufacturing function espouses strategy Y. Both sides invoke their expertise and experience to defend their assertions, and tempers sometimes rise. The first few times this happened, I managed to help the group muddle through the conflict.

Soon after, however, I added a new element to my planning workshops. Fairly early, we go through an exercise focused on a model of the enterprise—a depiction of how a typical company works. We discuss the group's company in terms of this model. Very often this leads to disagreements in the group about how the company actually does function. While these disagreements are not always resolved, they are at least now explicit. Consequently, planning proceeds much more smoothly.

This exercise is of value because much of the conflict between, for instance, strategies X and Y is due to the different functions' having different mental models of how the enterprise functions, both internally and in relation to its markets. In effect, marketing and manufacturing, in this example, are advocating strategies for different companies, as reflected in their different mental models. Making these differences explicit helps to lessen disagreements, or at least make them clear, and thereby enables moving beyond the potential deadlock.

On a more personal level, your mental models strongly affect what you look at, what information you seek, what you expect to happen, and how you explain what has happened. In these ways, your mental models can strongly affect how you interact with other people, both personally and professionally.

Do you expect people to be open to your ideas, or do you anticipate they will be hostile? If they endorse your ideas, do you accept this endorsement as genuine or do you see a hidden agenda? If they reject your ideas, do you try to understand their misgivings or do you, again, see a hidden agenda?

How does your enterprise function? What are the mechanisms for getting ahead in your career? What is the role of networking? What is the balance between style and substance? Who are role models for you?

What really counts in the marketplace where you pursue business? For example, do quality and service lead to easier subsequent sales? Is it possible to develop collaborative relationships with customers and other stakeholders, or are arm's-length relationships the norm?

These types of personal and professional questions can be difficult to answer. Nevertheless, by attempting to answer them, you can gain important insights into your mental models. In the context of this chapter on life planning, four types of models are of most interest. One type of model concerns your understanding of your own abilities, limitations, and inclinations. A second type of model involves interpersonal relationships. Another type of model relates to your relationships with organizations. The fourth type of model concerns the relationships that you and your current or potential organization have with your marketplace and society in general. Thus, there are personal, interpersonal, organizational, and societal models.

BELIEF SYSTEMS

In my experience, exploration of your mental models is best pursued in the context of a broader pursuit of an understanding of your needs and beliefs. This exploration can be conceptualized as filling in the matrix shown in Figure 7.1. Filling in this matrix constitutes a personal audit that serves as a precursor to planning.

You can fill in the elements of this matrix to represent your needs and beliefs—your belief system—in general, or you can fill in one matrix for your current life situation and one for the type of life you seek. I hasten to note that you should not expect that your personal belief system will change substantially because you pursue new directions in life. Your belief system may, however, change after a period of nurturing.

	Personal	Interpersonal	Organizational	Societal
Situational Needs				
Dispositional Needs				
Expectations				
Attributions				
Mental Models				

Figure 7.1   Belief System Matrix

What can you do with these insights once you have compiled them? The basic idea is to formulate life plans that meet your needs and are consistent with your beliefs. Further, your life plans should enable constructive evolution of your needs and beliefs. Thus, this personal audit helps you to understand whose life you are planning. You are not planning for the generic "economic man" who has all the standard desires, anxieties, and inclinations. You are planning for a specific, particular individual—you.

This type of personal audit has value beyond its use as a basis for planning. It can help you to understand your current situation and diagnose sources of stress. For example, you may have a strong need to achieve, as well as a moderate need for affiliation. However, you may have recently been promoted to a management position where a high need for power and a low need for affiliation are keys to success. If you are feeling uncomfortable and/or performing poorly, this mismatch may be the reason.

It may be possible to fill in the rows and columns of the belief system matrix by yourself, perhaps by addressing the numerous questions posed earlier in this chapter. However, people often have difficulties being honest with themselves. Also, people inherently have very biased views of themselves. For these reasons, it can be useful to have help. One possibility for help is your spouse or a friend. Another possibility is a professional psychologist or career counselor who, as noted earlier, is likely to have a variety of instruments for assessing the types of information needed to fill in the matrix.

Of course, there is no reason that you have to complete such an assessment all at once. You can discover your needs and beliefs over time. As I noted in Chapter 4, I discovered my need to create slack for myself while attempting to climb Mt. Rainier. This discovery was due, in part, to my being aware of myself in terms of needs and beliefs. In this way, I continually refine and revise my belief system matrix.

PLANNING FRAMEWORK

Once you have the initial understanding of yourself that an audit provides, you are ready to begin planning. This planning need not be pursued using a detailed, proceduralized methodology—in fact, I have none to offer. Instead, I suggest that you consider a few basic issues.

The first of these issues concerns envisioning alternatives and their consequences. It is important that you focus, at least initially, on what you would like rather than limiting yourself to what you imagine is possible. What knowledge and skills would you like to possess? What types of relationships do you desire? What type of organization would you like to create, or at least be part of? What role in society do you want—how do you want to add value?

These are very difficult questions. It is easy to avoid them. However, to do so risks the possibility that later in life, perhaps not much later, you will be among the aforementioned 60 percent to 90 percent of the people who feel disappointed, who feel that life has not worked out as they expected.

I have found a particularly useful way to address these questions. Simply choose any profession and/or type of organization. Next, imagine yourself in this job and type of organization. Perform a mental simulation. What is everyday life like? If you are not sure, ask someone in this profession or type of organization.

Using the "data" you collect in this exercise, compare these results to your belief system matrix. Will this future be compatible with your needs and beliefs? If not, what are the conflicts? Are there any variations of this profession or type of organization that do not have these conflicts? If there are, run the mental simulation again imagining yourself in this new situation.

If you go through this exercise for all possible professions, relationships, and organizations, you will be very, very old before you reach any conclusions. Thus, use your intuition to limit the search. My experience is that most people have only a handful of alternatives that they find at all appealing. Not even students want to consider such a broad range of alternatives as laborer, lawyer, librarian, linotype operator, liposuctionist, lion tamer, and lutist.

This exercise is particularly interesting for people who are in established positions and contemplating their possible futures. There is a tendency to focus on the next rung up the ladder, which may involve two or three possible positions. This is a very limited way of thinking.

Rather than focusing solely on the possibilities of becoming the next vice president of R&D, why not consider going back to the lab as a bench-level researcher? Why not leave your Fortune 500 company and start your own business? Why not leave and spend all your time sailing—like you have imagined doing on those shimmering September evenings when you have sailed through an orange drenched sunset?

I am not suggesting that you actually pursue these alternatives. I am advocating, however, that you *imagine* yourself pursuing them. Run the mental simulations. Imagine, in detail, what everyday life would be like if you pursued these alternatives. Don't think about them in terms of what you would escape. Think about them in terms of what you would gain.

Perhaps you will find one of these alternatives more and more appealing as you imagine it in increasing detail. More likely, you will find most of these alternatives less appealing as you get into the nitty-gritty of being in those situations day in and day out. In either case, you will have learned more about your possible futures.

Why go through this exercise? There are two primary reasons. First, if the result is that you dismiss these once attractive alternatives as no longer appealing because, for example, they are not compatible with your belief system, you will be much more comfortable pouring your energies into becoming the next vice president of R&D. You will not have to wistfully look in the rearview mirror at the roads not taken.

Second, you may find that one of the alternatives is very appealing. Perhaps the consulting business seems more and more attractive as you gather more information and run repeated mental simulations. On the one hand, this is great. You have identified the future you really want. On the other hand, this may be very inconvenient if you are saddled with huge mortgage payments and substantial college tuition bills for your children. Perhaps you should just "stick to the knitting" and win that promotion?

Why not do both? Why don't you work for the promotion and plan your consulting business? Does this sound like a prescription for frustration? It needn't be. Think in terms of evolutionary architectures.

The vision—Level C—is captured in some representation of you and your consulting business. The baseline—Level A—is the position of vice president of R&D. Your pursuit of Level A is planned in light of your Level C aspirations. Thus, you want to assure that the knowledge, skills, and relationships that you gain in attaining Level A have future value for Level C.

Level B—the bridging concept—can provide a vehicle for assuring the futurity of Level A relative to Level C. For example, I am familiar with several large companies whose R&D functions provide consulting services to their operating units. Perhaps your Level B aspirations can be the creation and growth of a first-rate consulting function within your R&D organization.

Interestingly, if you do this, you will be in the consulting business, even though you will remain within a big company—actually, you can view the company as a captive market for your consulting services. You may eventually decide that you can continue to pursue Level C without leaving the company. On the other hand, you may end up leaving. You do not have to decide that now. The focus now should be on achieving Level A and planning Level B.

A key in using the evolutionary architectures construct in this way involves applying two central principles to your life planning. One of these principles says, in a nutshell, that there should be a straightforward evolutionary path from A to B to C. Thus, the knowledge, skills, and relationships needed for Level A should be a subset of those needed for Level B, which are, in turn, a subset of those needed for Level C.

The second principle, stated in a personal form, says that you should intrigue yourself with Level C, market yourself Level B, and sell yourself Level A. Thus, the vision—Level C—should be compelling to you, not people in general, just you. Marketing yourself Level B involves motivating yourself to make the commitments necessary for the next big step on your life path. Selling yourself Level A simply means that you convince yourself to take the first step on your path.

There is another simple construct that complements the idea of evolutionary life plans. The basic idea is to think about your professional life in terms of four 10-year careers. The possibility of four distinct careers provides a wealth of opportunities for evolving from A to B to C.

To illustrate, my first 10-year career was as a professor of engineering, primarily in two large universities. My next 10-year career was as CEO of a contract R&D company. My third and current 10-year career involves helping a wide range of enterprises to recognize needs for fundamental changes and develop plans for these changes that they can confidently execute.

The fourth 10-year career is a bit open at the moment. I do not need a plan for perhaps four to six years. I have thought about it a bit, however. An idea that appeals to me very much is starting a small business involved with designing and manufacturing fine furniture. In light of the discussions in Chapter 2, this notion is probably not very surprising.

Yet, there does seem to be a disconnect. The first three 10-year careers seem to involve an evolutionary continuum, while this possible fourth career seems like more of a tangent. To an extent, this is true and, consequently, my fourth career may not involve woodworking. On the other hand, perhaps from a different point of view, woodworking would not be a tangent at all. This different point of view is discussed in Chapter 8.

The power of the 10-year construct lies in the fact that its essence is change. We used to view a career as something you selected, toiled in for 40 years, and then left for the balmy breezes of retirement. This construct suggests that this cycle can be repeated at least four times, with each career compressed into about a decade.

Why 10 years? Why not 5 or 15? The answer is simple. A variety of studies has shown that it takes about 10 years to become an expert in a domain. In the process of gaining this expertise, you are likely to make a variety of creative contributions. After the 10 years, however, I think your prospects for making important contributions are diminished, in part because you know too much. It's time to take your expertise and move on to new challenges where the renewed need to learn will open new possibilities for creative insights and ideas.

The possibility of four 10-year careers inherently implies change. Inherent change can be supported and facilitated by planning. The envisioning portion of this planning can be accomplished using the idea of evolutionary architectures. You can use the prospects of four distinct careers as a means for pursuing Level A and subsequently Level B, as well as the vehicle for advancing toward the ultimate of Level C.

CHOICE AND COMMITMENT

Envisioning is important, but it is not enough. The next step is choice and commitment. Few of us would start cutting wood or hiking a trail without a sense of what we were going to build or where we were trying to go. However, this happens frequently in people's lives. People often fail to choose destinations.

While life planning should involve making choices and committing yourself to these choices, many people simply act and react opportunistically. They take the best job available. They acquire many possessions and responsibilities. They worry about the money needed to support these possessions and responsibilities. Over the years, many attractive paths are wistfully considered but, due to a lack of choice and commitment, none of these alternate paths are taken. Life just happens.

In my experience, this is due in part to people's avoiding making choices and avoiding making commitments to the choices they are willing to make. I have encountered many highly educated people in their thirties and forties who are not sure what they want to do in life. Whatever they are doing at the moment, they are doing without commitment because they are fairly, but not completely, sure that they do not want to continue on this path. They feel they have not gotten started yet.

Further, they are unwilling to choose because any particular choice might preclude other choices. For example, I regularly meet many people who are about to go back to school and earn Ph.D. degrees. Many of these people have been "about" to do this for several years. The longer they wait, the more frustrated they become.

Yet they cannot bring themselves to say yes or no. And life happens.

The importance of choice and commitment is best captured for me in an illustration by artist Mary Engelbreit. In this picture, a young girl is walking down a path with a stick over her shoulder carrying the traditional bundle on the end of the stick. She is also carrying a small suitcase. The girl has approached a fork in the road and is confidently headed down the left side of the fork.

The road sign at the fork she has just passed has two pieces. One piece points in the direction the girl is headed. This piece reads "Your Life." The other piece of the sign points in the direction of the right side of the fork, the road not taken. It reads "No Longer An Option." On the top of the picture is a banner that reads "Don't Look Back."

This picture is about choice and commitment. The girl has made her choice. She is committed to this choice. She is not looking back and wondering if she should have made other choices. She epitomizes a very important aspect of life planning. I have a copy of this picture hanging next to my bathroom sink at home and in my office at work.

An important aspect of life planning is time. Time plays a role in terms of our understanding and accepting stages of growth, rites of passage, and change in general. Part of this involves understanding that transitions take time. In any endeavor, it takes time to get beyond paying your dues and gain the ability to keep things in perspective.

Time also relates to timing. There is a time in your life to be a brash "young Turk" and later times when the role of leader, and eventually mentor and coach, is appropriate. For example, I have enjoyed the good fortune of having a variety of people, mostly men, look out for me in my early professional years and still have several of these types of relationships. I have found in recent years, however, that it is time for me to help others to hike, to look out for others in terms of pointing out opportunities and trying to help them to seize these opportunities.

To an extent, understanding the role of time in life planning requires a keen sense for the unfolding plot of your story and the larger and longer stories within which you are playing, or might play, roles. As you pursue your second, and then third, 10-year career, you begin to see how your roles fit in the broader scheme of things, as well as how you fit in these roles. Time and timing help you to gain this perspective and to take advantage of it.

Relationships

Relationships are also a key issue. Relationships cut across the personal, interpersonal, organizational, and societal aspects of our lives. As we plan our lives and pursue our personal and professional goals, we often attempt to control these relationships. We tend to focus on making things happen. Yet, what is needed is collaboration across these types of relationships. Life does not have to be a zero-sum game. It can be a collaborative undertaking.

However, life planning can create a central tension in relationships. Overemphasis on the integration and authenticity of personal plans can undermine the pursuit of inclusivity. In other words, defining your own personal story can conflict with immersing yourself in the larger and longer stories of humankind. Creative balancing of this tension is an important life-planning skill.

This skill can easily take decades to develop, and, along the way, life may be littered with bruised and broken relationships as you pursue your visions. Alternatively, your vision can explicitly include consideration of relationships. In this way, your life plans are unlikely to include only your life.

To an extent, you can actually plan relationships. This is most evident in creating an enterprise. Planning the life of an enterprise involves all the elements of planning discussed thus far in this chapter. By understanding the existing belief systems in an organization—its collective needs and beliefs—you can mold a vision that will work for the organization in the sense that the changes portrayed and planned will meet collective needs and be supportive of collective beliefs. In this way, you are planning and designing a set of relationships.

I hasten to note that this is best pursued in a collaborative manner. Leading an organization, especially a young growing organization, is akin to sailing. You have to understand the winds and take advantage of this understanding, perhaps taking many tacks in the process of pursuing your vision. You may think that you can power your way forward, hands on the open throttle, breaking through waves and fighting the wind head on. You can't, at least you can't for very long. For long-term success, you have to learn to collaborate with the forces that affect your enterprise.

Resources

Thus far, we have ignored issues associated with the resources necessary for pursuing your vision (Level C), the baseline (Level A), and the bridging concept (Level B), perhaps via four or more 10-year careers. Can you really plan to become anything you want? Or do you have to consider the extent of your resources before you start envisioning alternative futures?

Obviously, at some point you have to consider these resources. What are your abilities and aptitudes? Are they appropriate and sufficient for pursuing your vision? What organizational resources can you call on? How can you assure that the organization will maintain its commitment to your plans?

My experience is that these types of questions often get asked too early. As a result, the answers to these question tend to become anchors on the planning process. I suggest a simple guideline. At first, focus all your attention on the desirability of your vision. Later, you can worry about its feasibility.

Many people have great difficulty following this guidance. They feel that they will become committed to ridiculous goals and subsequently determine that they have no chance of achieving them. For example, the 47-year-old, former high school basketball player might aspire to a career in the NBA, perhaps playing for the Boston Celtics. However, once Kareem Abdul Jabaar retired at the age of 42, when I was a slightly younger 42, I knew that my chances had disappeared.

I think that you should first be optimistic, then realistic, and never pessimistic. I have found that people tend to aspire to goals that require their knowledge and skills, or at least knowledge and skills they have the aptitude to gain. Further, there are ways you can enhance your chances of achieving success as you implement your plans—these suggestions are discussed later in this chapter.

Risks

Another planning issue concerns risk. How can you deal with the uncertainty associated with life planning? How can you feel secure in your plans? First of all, you cannot eliminate uncertainty. As I have noted in earlier discussions, I personally am thankful that life is full of uncertainties, surprises, and adventures.

Nevertheless, even if you embrace the adventure implied by your plans, all of us would like to feel secure in our plans. This begs the question of the meaning of security. This issue can be thought about on several levels.

One level concerns your sense of security in, for example, your company. Will your company prosper, and will there be good jobs available? Another level concerns your job. Will one of the available jobs be yours?

The most important level of security, I think, involves being secure in yourself. Do you know who you are? Do you know where you are going? Do you know how you are going to get there? Do you understand and accept the risks? The purpose of this chapter on life planning is to help you answer these questions.

Risks. What can go wrong? Well, obviously, you could lose your job. However, if you are secure in yourself, you are very likely to be confident in your abilities to find a new job.

What about loss of financial security? This is a very personal question. Here is what it means to me. A temporary setback—for example, being out of work for a month or two—might require that I skip vacation this year. A longer-term setback might require that I sell my house and rent again. Perhaps I might have to sell my car. Perhaps I would have to sell all the power tools in my workshop and all my hiking equipment. How bad could it really get? And—would I really let it happen?

Ten years ago, when our company was only a few years old, we opened a branch office on the West Coast. A friend and competitor, who had been in business many years, asked me, "Your company is so young. How can you take such a risk?"

I said, "The worst that can happen is that we go out of business, and I lose my house (which was pledged to the company's bank at that time)." I was going to do my best to avoid these conse-quences, but I could accept them. It may be that growing up poor—without our own house, car, TV, or vacations—has given me an advantage in this regard.

Loss of job and financial security is minor, in my opinion, compared to the greatest risk of all—losing your way! This involves losing track of who you are, where you are going, and how you are going to get there. This can result in great uncertainty, loss of self-esteem, and a lack of hope. However, if you know where you are going—and know yourself—the ultimate risks are very small.

Don't worry about failure. Decide what you want and how you might get there. If success seems very unlikely, perhaps you should reconsider. However, if you expect success to be almost guaranteed, you will never act. Keep in mind that in pursuing your goals, there are no failures, only temporary setbacks.

IMPLEMENTING PLANS

In order to realize your vision, you have to implement your plans. My experience is that good plans often fail because of poor imple-mentation or, in some cases, lack of implementation. After contrib-uting to and observing a variety of implementation problems, I developed a set of simple principles that can help to avoid such difficulties.

These principles also grew out of the recognition that plans can seldom be implemented unilaterally. Unless you are planning to become a hermit, successful implementation of plans depends on enlisting other stakeholders to buy into or at least support your plans. Stakeholders include your spouse and family, partners and employees, investors, customers, and so on.

Whether your plan is to become an artist, computer entrepre-neur, mountain climber, orchestra conductor, or woodworking teacher, you need the understanding and support of your stake-holders in order to succeed. Very few people succeed all on their own. The principles of plan implementation listed in Figure 7.2 are very much focused on understanding the conditions under which others will support your vision and plans.

- Look for a confluence of agendas.

- Clearly perceived is clearly expressed.

- Sell yourself as well as your vision and plans.

- Detailed planning works.

- Learn as you go.

- Focus on the goal.

- Delight your stakeholders.

Figure 7.2 Principles of Plan Implementation

The first principle is "Look for a confluence of agendas." The world does not exist for the purpose of supporting you and your plans. Other people have their own agendas within which you must fit. To do this you need two things.

First, obviously, you have to know your own agenda. Given that you have successfully resolved the types of issues discussed thus far in this chapter, you will clearly be well aware of your own agenda.

Second, you need to understand other stakeholders' agendas. What is important to them organizationally and personally? What benefits are they seeking to gain? What costs do they want to minimize or avoid? How will collaborating with you—by, for example, hiring you or buying your product—provide these benefits with agreeable costs?

With an understanding of your agenda and the agendas of other stakeholders, you should be able to identify confluences where everybody gets something they want. In such situations, stakeholders will view you as someone who can meet their needs. They will be predisposed to collaborating with you.

The next principle is "Clearly perceived is clearly expressed." If you really understand what you want to do, you should be able to communicate it clearly. If you cannot communicate, you do not understand. A few simple guidelines can help.

You should be able to provide a compelling description of your vision and plans in one or two pages of writing. What value added are you going to provide? What problems will you solve? What needs will you meet? What benefits will you create in order to support stakeholders' agendas?

You should also be able to provide evidence that you are capable of executing these plans and realizing the compelling vision you have described. Evidence can include your track record for delivering on promises. Thorough understanding of stakeholders' agendas also tends to be viewed as strong evidence.

You are now ready to "Sell yourself as well as your vision and plans." Stakeholders do not buy into visions and plans in isolation from the people advocating them. There are several elements of selling yourself.

Credibility is crucial. Not only do you need evidence that you can execute your plan, you also need to provide evidence of your overall merits. This can include your past accomplishments and endorsements by opinion leaders. From this perspective, a key subplan within your overall life plan is accumulation of experiences and successes that build your overall credibility.

I have also found that attitude can be a clincher. Be positive and optimistic. Ask questions. Listen carefully. Identify agendas. Don't be glib. Don't be defensive. Be honest and sincere.

Throughout the process of plan implementation, relationships are central. It is essential that you recognize that you are building relationships with other stakeholders, not just using their support to achieve your ends. Relationships take effort. Think carefully about how to establish and build relationships with existing and potential stakeholders.

A fourth principle is "Detailed planning works." Develop a detailed plan for building a constituency for your vision. This detailed plan should include consideration of who you are going to contact, how you are going to approach them, what questions you will ask, and how you plan to follow up.

In this process, cast a wide net. Think of as many potential stakeholders as you can. Ask your colleagues for ideas of who to contact. Use existing stakeholders as sources of new potential stakeholders. Pursue all these stakeholders in parallel.

Network from one potential stakeholder to another. Tell each of them why you are contacting them. Describe your vision briefly. Ask if they would like to see your written description. If not, ask them who might. Also ask what issues and problems are of most interest to them—such information might later prove to be very useful.

Schedule followups with stakeholders. Make a note in your calendar to follow up within a fixed period, say two weeks, after the initial contact. Ask them for their reactions to your agenda. Ask how it fits into their agenda. Ask if they will be willing to support your pursuits, perhaps with an investment but at least with an endorsement.

The next principle is "Learn as you go." It is very unlikely that existing or potential stakeholders are sitting and waiting for your particular vision and plans. Thus, you may have to adapt your agenda a bit to enable an intersection with theirs. To understand what adaptations are needed, it is very useful to study stakeholders' current activities and intentions, perhaps using the methods and tools of the naturalist phase.

In this process, make sure that every contact is a sale, at least of you. You are not only trying to convince people to support the specific plan you have in hand, you are also marketing yourself to gain support for future plans, perhaps plans that are mutations of your current plan.

With every interaction, you should be adding a node to your network or increasing your knowledge about existing nodes. Until this process becomes natural, almost instinctual, try actually drawing the network with organizational and personal links.

Use every opportunity—all feedback, both positive and negative—to improve your vision and evolve your plans. Don't let your ego get in the way. Reflect upon people's reactions. Analyze the implications of adapting to their suggestions. My assumption in such analyses is that the world is smart and I am less than fully informed. This is a bit simplistic, but it lowers defense mechanisms and opens me to improving my plans.

The sixth principle is "Focus on the goal." Don't forget that your goal is to advance your plan and gain the opportunity to pursue it fully. Networking and relationship building can be very enjoyable elements of your life. Many of these relationships will come to have value far beyond the purpose of advancing your plans. However, do not lose sight of your goals.

It is important to commit to the "quest." In many ways, commitment and endurance are more important than having the world's best vision and plans. Think in terms of vision, mission, and calling, not just career building. If you are worried about failing, don't forget that the best way to avoid failure is to not act. Of course, this requires that you forego potential accomplishments.

You can make success inevitable. With a good plan and a lot of energy, you will succeed. If necessary, turn over every stone and follow every lead. With the right attitude, there are no failures—only temporary setbacks.

If opportunities and resources are slow in coming, start pursuing your plan on your own. A typical work week consumes a bit over 20 percent of your time. Sleep takes roughly 30 percent. With 50 percent left, you should be able to devote 2 percent to 3 percent to your quest. Five *quality* hours per week can, over time, produce amazing results.

The final principle is "Delight your stakeholders." Stakeholders are not just purveyors of support. Once implementation of your plan is underway, do not ignore them until you need more support. Try to delight them with your evolving success.

Make sure that stakeholders are aware of what you are doing and have reasonable expectations. Talk to them about problems and tough decisions. Call them when exciting progress is made.

If things go wrong, don't worry about whose fault it is. Assume that it's your fault, fix the problem, and move on. It is easier if it is your fault because then you can do something about it. Further, the "bottom line" is always that you have to solve the problem because it's your vision and your plans.

Try to deliver more than you promised. Nothing is better for assuring continued support than your exceeding stakeholders' expectations. Further, use every opportunity for stakeholders to get as much credit as possible for what you have accomplished. Once they develop a sense of ownership, they will invest themselves in helping you to advance what has now become a mutual vision and shared plans.

These seven principles for plan implementation are very simple, almost intuitive. However, they are also very powerful. Using them can enable you to get more and more stakeholders to buy into your vision and plans. In the process, if you are able to be open, they will contribute to elaborating and improving the vision and plans. In this way, life planning becomes a collaborative process whereby everybody participates in writing the script of the story that you have mutually invested yourselves in creating.

IMPORTANT INGREDIENTS

I have found that there are three other critical, yet subtle, ingredients in discovery and life planning: patience, persistence, and passion. Patience is needed because good things often take time. Some of my personal goals have taken 20 years to achieve. I am hoping that some of my corporate goals will be realized a bit faster. Nevertheless, the time frame for successfully executing important components of life plans is at least years and, more likely, substantial fractions of decades.

Persistence is needed because plans can be thwarted and not work out as intended. Assumptions may turn out to not have been warranted. The market climate may change. Technology breakthroughs may occur. You should persist in executing your plans as long as they make sense. If they no longer make sense, you should reconsider your vision and plans.

This may require seeking other possibilities via modified or perhaps new paths. It is important to keep in mind that plans are not promises. Plans are simply an informed consensus for achieving mutual goals. As such, plans should be open for modification as results emerge and lessons are learned.

The passions of woodworking, hiking, and discovery were discussed in earlier chapters. Discovery not only helps you to see the passions in others—it provides an avenue for forming and understanding your own passions. Pursuit of these passions should be embodied in your vision and plans.

In some cases, this process of internal discovery not only leads to understanding of your passions, it can also lead to personal insights that may or may not be desirable. Fortunately, however, negative discoveries can lead to positive change. There is no guarantee that discoveries will all be positive. You can, however, be reasonably assured that personal discoveries will lead to change.

The opposite of patient and persistent passions is fickle and frantic flirtations. I frequently encounter people who have no vision and no plans. Their lives appear to be a series of flirtations. They are going to go back to graduate school, start a business, become missionaries, retire on the job while they hone their sailing skills. A few months later, there may be a new agenda.

I find that people with this orientation tend to be fickle and often change the objects of their flirtations. In the midst of a flirtation, they are often frantic in their ardor. They want to achieve success immediately. If they fail to succeed quickly, they abandon the current flirtation to seek another.

This type of behavior is, in my opinion, predictable in teenagers, understandable in young adults, possibly acceptable for those in their late twenties and early thirties, but pitiful for those who are older. I am not saying that career changes—or totally new adventures—in middle age are pitiful. I am saying that being 35 or 40 years old and never having made any substantive commitments is pitiful. It is pitiful because life just happens. The wealth of time that you have, in Joseph Campbell's words, to find your bliss gets shorter and shorter. There is no reason to waste this precious resource.

My conclusion is that people in such situations do not see their roles in broader contexts and, consequently, pursue no real passions. They experiment and sample the buffet of life. In jumping from one flirtation to another, their lives may slowly mutate.

However, they do not consciously change and grow. They do not become adult in Erik Erikson's sense of the term.

The alternative path is not necessarily one that focuses on planning. The first step is probably one of discovery—a naturalist phase, if you will, with yourself as the object of study. This can begin with external discovery by placing yourself in circumstances where you have no choice but to discover the world in which you are immersed. This can set the stage—provide the venue for being open—for internal discovery.

By being open to the surprises and likely changes due to internal discoveries, life plans can be framed and slowly elaborated. For me, a key discovery has been the role of writing in my life. Over the past 20+ years, I have written or edited many books and hundreds of articles. I now realize that writing is the way I understand and communicate my story. Woodworking, hiking, and discovery are the ways I create my story.

SUMMARY

In light of all the issues, processes, and methods discussed in this chapter, what is life planning? I think that it is much simpler than I may have been able to portray in this chapter. At the risk of over-simplifying, I will offer a very simple prescription.

The first step of life planning involves assessing your needs and beliefs. What situational and dispositional needs affect your behavior? What expectations, attributions, and mental models influence your perceptions of the world?

The next step relates to envisioning alternatives and their consequences. This requires that you free yourself from the often mundane reality of today and allow yourself to picture what you desire without worrying about how you will succeed in these pursuits. Mental simulations can help you to imagine the likely consequences of your visions.

Given all of your images of the future, as well as the likely consequences of these images, the next step concerns formulating an evolutionary architecture that embodies and balances the short term and the long term. This formulation should capture the sense of where you are ultimately headed, as well as of what will happen tomorrow and over the next months.

The next step is choice and commitment. At some point, you simply have to choose and then do your best to make it happen. There is no longer room for analysis. There is only room for decision making and commitment to a specific course of action. At this point there are no regrets, only energy directed toward making the vision real.

The emphasis shifts to implementation. Understanding stakeholders and relationships becomes central. You are selling yourself as well as your vision and plans. Your goal is to get as many people as possible to, in effect, add your life goals and plans to their personal agendas. They are not being altruistic. You have succeeded in finding a confluence of agendas.

The whole process of life planning works best if it is supported by a foundation of patience, persistence, and passion. In this situation, I have found that potential stakeholders feel that they have no choice but to listen to you. They have little choice but to support you. They have no better choices but to sign on to your compelling agenda.

What does this all mean? Is the success of your life plans assured? No. Earnest and studious reflection, as well as thoughtful and prudent planning, cannot guarantee success. However, adopting the philosophy advocated in this chapter, and pursuing the planning scheme described in this chapter, can assure that you place yourself in the path or, better yet, at the crossroads of serendipity.

If life planning only succeeds at this, while also preparing you to recognize serendipity when it arises, planning will have proven its value. Best laid plans may be delayed and thwarted. But grief and pain will have been averted, and promised joy will, eventually, be a reality.

8

Transformation and Growth

Transformation and growth are processes involving cycles of awareness, knowledge, understanding, skill, enlightenment, and transcendence.

Transformation and growth were recurrent themes in the discussions of woodworking, hiking, and discovery, as well as in the consideration of product, business, and life plans. Regardless of the clarity with which the processes of transformation and growth are explained, they nonetheless remain a struggle. Planning is not a natural act. Planning requires determination and persistence if it is to pay off.

To an extent, methodologies and tools can help to ease the burden of planning. However, the real value of the planning methodologies discussed in Chapters 3, 5, and 7 is in the philosophy and practices that they promote rather than the specific steps per se. In particular, openness, collaboration, facilitation, and other aspects of these planning processes are what makes them work. The methodologies and tools can be catalysts for transformation and growth, but they do not embody such changes in themselves.

UNDERLYING CYCLE

I find it useful to think of transformation and growth as a cycle. This cycle involves six steps that wind back upon themselves in a manner similar to an Escher drawing. In this way, the cycle repeats itself, although it broadens with each cycle.

The first step is *awareness*. You become aware of, for example, a primitive culture in a developing country. This awareness prompts you to study this culture by, for instance, reading books. This leads to *knowledge*. Perhaps this knowledge leads you to visit this country and begin to gain *understanding* of this culture.

Possibly you are further motivated to live in this country for a year or more. As you immerse yourself in the culture, you start to develop *skill* in living as part of this culture. After 5 to 10 years, your perceptions of this society have matured to the point of *enlightenment*. You now see how it all fits together—why things are the way they are and why people value them that way. With enough study and experience, you may begin to see this culture as part of a greater scheme, a larger whole. The result may be *transcendence*, whereby your focus is now broadened and heightened. You are now aware of a larger context, and the cycle begins again.

Understanding this cycle enables us to transform representations of problems and to see alternative paths for realizing our visions. Beyond transforming problems, knowledge of this cycle can lead to transformation of our views of our roles. These two types of transformations can facilitate dealing creatively with thwarted and/or disappointing plans. With patience, persistence, and passion, we can embrace change with much greater intentionality.

Recognizing the existence of this cycle, as well as understanding where you are at any point in time, can provide a strong basis for integration and authenticity as discussed in earlier chapters. In this chapter, these conclusions are illustrated in the context of three stories. The first story concerns the path whereby my interests and activities evolved from engineering design to enterprises as a whole. The second story relates to my evolving sense of the role and value of planning. Finally, I briefly consider why, for me, going into the fine-furniture business would be a reasonable and consistent fourth 10-year career.

MOVING UP IN LEVELS OF AGGREGATION

When I first encountered courses on systems theory and systems engineering as an undergraduate, I became fascinated. During my junior and senior years, I worked part time in systems engineering for a large defense contractor. The die was cast. I would henceforth always be concerned with the "big picture."

In graduate school, I became intrigued with a particular aspect of systems, namely, the people within them. I became aware of the centrality of human behavior to the functioning of systems. Graduate school then became a quest to gain knowledge in this area, as well as the skills necessary to understanding and solving human-related problems from a systems-oriented perspective.

Throughout graduate studies and as an engineering faculty member for many years, in conjunction with my colleagues, I studied operators and maintainers of complex systems. In particular, we focused on aircraft pilots, process plant operators, aircraft mechanics, and military operations and maintenance personnel. We gained understanding of their abilities and limitations, as well as of how to support them via training and aiding.

As our set of experiences broadened, we began to wonder why the human interfaces within systems were often designed so poorly. It seemed that much of the knowledge necessary to yield better interfaces was readily available. Why wasn't this information accessed and utilized?

This question led us to explore the nature of design. Our focus shifted to designers rather than operators and maintainers. We became enlightened in the sense that we realized that we had to understand and directly influence designers if we hoped that better systems would be created for operators and maintainers.

This caused us to devote several years to studying designers' activities in general and their information-seeking activities in particular. We learned that designers of, for example, aircraft cockpits need a wealth of information and have very little time to access and utilize this information. We also learned that very little of the published research results concerning how to support the performance of operators and maintainers is ever accessed by

designers. They find it difficult to understand the practical implications of this material and generally judge it to be irrelevant.

Designers tend to get most of their information from colleagues. This source is "good enough" relative to the time and cost
necessary for accessing and utilizing more formal sources. This
conclusion led us to focus on repackaging research results into
easy-to-use methods and tools. This generated much interest.
However, adoption of these methods and tools was slow because,
we found, adoption required the consent and support of management.

We again became enlightened and our perspective broadened.
To affect design in any fundamental way, we would have to understand the broader business context within which design functions.
This led us to focus on business practices and the ways in which
companies plan and design new products, as well as how they
form business strategies around these offerings. A new set of easy-
to-use methods and tools emerged to support these activities.

Frequent interaction with top management groups, as well as
with various task forces and committees, led to another phase of
enlightenment and broadening awareness. Enterprises are not
free to adopt whatever business practices they might desire. They
are strongly affected by the markets, as well as the communities
and society, within which they operate. Enterprises have broader
roles, at least as employers but also as contributors to the common
good. Thus, for example, they have to be socially and environmen-
tally conscious.

My mental model of how to support operators and maintainers of systems has gone through much transformation and
growth. It started by gaining understanding of these types of jobs
and the people who typically perform them. It next broadened to
consider the people who design systems and, in effect, also design
the jobs within these systems. It broadened again to include the
organizations that employ these designers. This led to consideration of how enterprises chart their futures, as well as of how they
function in society. This transformation and growth has greatly
improved our abilities to affect change because we are continually
improving our understanding of the roles and interests of all the
players—the stakeholders—in the big picture.

This story illustrates transformation and growth by broadening the scope of the problem space within which issues are viewed. This broadened view is highly aggregated in that each piece of the current puzzle was formerly viewed as a whole puzzle in itself. In this way, this process of transformation and growth can be thought of as moving up in levels of aggregation.

MOVING UP IN LEVELS OF ABSTRACTION

Another, complementary, approach to transformation and growth involves moving up in levels of abstraction. To illustrate this type of process, the next story concerns my evolving sense of the role and value of planning. To begin, I should admit that I am inherently a planner. More specifically, I have always been a dreamer and schemer. Most of my dreams and schemes are never actually pursued—which is probably fortunate—but a few have worked out fairly well.

My introduction to planning in a formal sense occurred when I worked in the construction industry as a teenager. You need an explicit plan if you are going to build, wire, plumb, and paint a house. Certain sequences of activities work much better than the many other possibilities. For example, wiring and plumbing should occur after the wall studs are in place, but before the drywall.

My education and experience as a systems engineer also included a heavy dose of planning. My first engineering job with a large defense contractor introduced me to project planning, work breakdown structures, and so on. At that time, I conceptualized planning as a process of defining activities and precedence relationships among activities, determining the resources (e.g., people, facilities, time) required by these activities, and projecting profiles of resources consumed as well as milestone dates.

As noted earlier, I subsequently focused on the roles, abilities, and limitations of people in systems. This included numerous studies of problem solving and planning in air-traffic control, aviation, process control, maintenance, and other domains. We found that people in these types of environments rarely plan in the manner just described. In contrast, people's behavior is governed by standard or routine "scripts" they follow until events or patterns of system behaviors cause them to realize that the current script is not working.

Often the standard scripts are so well learned that people require a tremendous amount of evidence before they are willing to make a change. Their first tactic is likely to be one of searching, in their heads, for some other standard script that now applies. Only in the last resort will people pursue the type of analytical planning portrayed earlier.

Why are people like this? I think that the answer is simple— it works. Actually, it works most of the time, but not all of the time. For familiar and frequent situations, it works very well and very efficiently. For familiar and infrequent situations, it can work well, but is often inefficient. However, for unfamiliar and inherently infrequent situations, script-driven behaviors are often inappropriate, and more formal planning is needed.

I have found that this characterization of types of planning also fits business planning. Over the past 10+ years, I have discovered in business, first my own and then many others, how difficult planning can be. Our studies of difficulties in product and business planning led us to identify the three problems discussed in Chapter 1, namely, that people do not know what to do, that what they choose to do often takes a very long time, and that when they get done they do not have anything they value. Various methods of training and aiding can help to overcome these difficulties.

Another way to avoid planning difficulties is to avoid planning. Many enterprises, particularly large enterprises, tend to get trapped in their dominant scripts. Another way of saying this is that companies get trapped by their dominant metaphors. For example, aircraft companies approach all problems as if they were aircraft design problems. Electronics companies approach all problems as if they were electronics design problems. There are many other similar examples.

Difficulties arise when the dominant metaphors no longer apply. Enterprises can delude themselves for years until the marketplace or their constituency gives them a major shock. Suddenly, they scramble, almost in panic, to adapt to the new environment that has been evolving around them for years without their realizing it.

From this perspective, two different types of planning occur in enterprises. The most prevalent type I would term budgeting rather than planning. People assume, perhaps implicitly, that the future will be very much like the past, only there will be more sales, profits, people, and so on. For this type of planning, the resulting plans are mainly tabulations of numbers.

The other type of planning has been the focus of this book. It is driven by a need to change rather than simply to do more of the same things, perhaps faster or cheaper. My experience is that enterprises have great difficulty recognizing that they need to do this type of planning. Further, even when key people have recognized this need, it may be very difficult to build a consensus among all the members of the organization.

I have found that major crises are the best way to precipitate broader recognition of the need to change. For this reason, it can be useful to avoid averting inevitable crises. Instead, you can enter a crisis willingly, knowing that the shock will help the enterprise to transform itself, earlier rather than later, and begin to grow again. Planning then becomes the means to creating change.

This is a very different view of planning from the project planning/budgeting view discussed earlier. The planning process, not just the resulting plans, can provide the means for addressing and resolving fundamental needs for change. In this way, planning can be a catalyst for transformation and growth. The result is not only plans, but also confidence and, hopefully, consensus about the enterprise's aspirations and expectations.

Thus, my view of planning has been transformed and has grown to include more abstract purposes for planning. My view is no longer limited to activities, resources, and so forth. My view has broadened to include conceptual elements such as change, confidence, and consensus.

I have also come to realize that there are many situations where planning is not necessary. There are situations where you can simply be opportunistic. For example, there may be many alternatives, and you may not be sure of the feasibility and/or desirability of each alternative. If the cost of experimenting is very low or at least acceptable, opportunistic pursuit of these alternatives may be a reasonable strategy.

This strategy is typical for technology-oriented new businesses. These types of businesses often begin with an emphasis on selling technical services, possibly as a means of bootstrapping themselves toward eventual product offerings. Opportunistic pursuit of a wide range of projects provides such firms with increased understanding of potential markets, greater experience for their personnel, and, of course, cash flow.

There are opportunity costs associated with a lack of focus and, consequently, a lack of plans. However, these costs may be acceptable if the nascent enterprise has no compelling vision. In fact, I have found that requirements to produce plans can be quite stressful to those who have yet to formulate their vision.

I am by no means advocating that planning be omitted. I am simply recognizing that planning can be premature. Nevertheless, if only to pay the bills, people have to act whether or not they have plans. The key, I think, is to develop a commitment to gain sufficient understanding and experience to eventually transform and grow the enterprise via a well-articulated vision and corresponding plans. Otherwise, the enterprise is likely to remain perpetually in a hand-to-mouth mode.

Finally, as noted earlier, I have come to realize that plans inevitably are not executed exactly as anticipated. Thus, they are not like road maps that have to be followed without deviation. Instead, they are maps that, at the very least, should place you in the path or, better yet, at the crossroads, of serendipity.

This story of how my view of planning has changed illustrates transformation and growth by moving up in levels of abstraction. The transformation and growth did not involve a broadening of the scope of planning as it did in the earlier story. Instead, it involved a broadening of the set of abstractions with which planning can be viewed. These abstractions include activities, resources, change, confidence, consensus, opportunism, and serendipity. In this way, planning has become a much richer construct.

CREATING COMPELLING MODELS

My third story of transformation and growth involves a brief explanation of why woodworking would be a plausible and consistent choice for my fourth 10-year career. My first career in academia was primarily a time of learning, via research studies, about people's abilities and limitations in tasks typically performed in complex systems. The second career, heading a contract R&D company, involved applying this knowledge while also learning about how to run a business. My third career involves applying this business knowledge to helping a wide variety of enterprises while also learning about how best to teach, coach, and mentor people who want to apply the methods and tools discussed throughout this book.

It seems to me that a reasonable next step is to create a compelling model of the application of all this knowledge. This model should involve a real enterprise that is in business to provide a down-to-earth concrete product that almost anyone can understand and appreciate. This model should be a microcosm where all the concepts, principles, methods, and tools can be fully implemented and illustrated.

I should note that my current company, which focuses on software products and systems, does not fully fit the bill as a compelling model. Software is too abstract for many people. Further, manufacturing of software is not representative of manufacturing in general. Finally, a business where most of the employees have M.S. degrees or higher is not at all typical. The needed model must be such that everyone can imagine themselves as part of this enterprise.

I can imagine many readers saying, "This woodworking business sounds like an interesting idea, but where is the transformation and growth?" The compelling change, for me, is the sense of how best to package awareness, knowledge, understanding, skill, enlightenment, and transcendence. In my first career, this packaging involved articles in research journals. I naively thought that good research results would quickly affect practice. I discovered, however, that the only readers of those articles were other researchers.

By starting a company, we were able to transition research results into practice more quickly. Our software products and systems reflect the understanding gained in past and ongoing research. The difficulty is that this provides very little leverage beyond our products and services. The design community in general is affected only very slowly and indirectly.

Helping others to plan and design new products and ventures broadens the impact but still is limited to a slowly growing network. What is needed is a means to empower people to transform and grow the ways in which they design their products and systems. Methods and tools are important elements of this means.

I now realize that a critical additional element is one or more concrete, compelling examples or models that embody the essence of the philosophy, principles, and practices of human-centered design. I think that a woodworking business could provide such a model. While I used to focus on authoring research articles, and more recently emphasized authoring books and associated software products, I now see that it may be time to author companies to provide the compelling models that are needed. This transformation from *word*working to *wood*working could enable creation of a compelling story of how to apply human-centered design.

The chances are that serendipity will intervene, and I will never go into the woodworking business and have the opportunity to create this model. Nevertheless, it is a compelling possibility to me at the moment. At the very least, this vision has helped me to understand how philosophies, principles, practices, and so on, can best be packaged to assure that people will be compelled to explore and experiment with new ways of thinking.

THE CONTEXT OF PLANNING

To close, it is important to consider the question "What about things other than planning?" This question typically reflects two concerns. One of these concerns is the need to view planning in a broader context. Planning is part of a process that includes both upstream and downstream activities.

Upstream activities are those associated with understanding current and likely future situations, as well as changes that may be needed to assure that the future is as desired. Situation assessment, in terms of both seeking information and formulating explanations, is a critical precursor of planning and committing to implementing plans.

Downstream activities involve execution of plans and monitoring of their progress. Many good plans fail because of poor execution. In some cases, plans are not fully implemented. In other cases, plan execution is not carefully monitored, resulting, for example, in situations where market assumptions are no longer true, but execution proceeds without reconsideration.

Thus, inadequate or incorrect situation assessment and/or execution and monitoring can result in best laid plans' yielding grief and pain rather than promised joy. Why does this happen? My experience is that this is often because the status quo is overwhelmingly compelling, particularly in large enterprises.

This reflects a failure to transform and grow continually. The cycle of awareness, knowledge, understanding, skill, enlightenment, and transcendence is broken. Enterprises become stalled, typically at a point where they are highly skilled at what they do but unenlightened concerning the decreasing competitive advantage provided by these skills. This phenomenon is also common for individuals. In both cases, timely and hopefully early crises may precipitate reenergizing of the cycle of transformation and growth.

The second way in which the question about things beyond planning arises concerns the relative value of planning compared to laying back and smelling the roses. This type of question implies that I spend most of my time planning. It also implies that the person asking the question cannot imagine devoting that much time to planning.

I actually spend a very modest amount of time planning personally, as well as leading the planning process in my company. However, I spend considerable time helping others to plan and, in particular, to create good plans quickly. I know that planning does not have to be overwhelming. Further, I have found that the process of planning and implementing your plans is often as rewarding as the "prizes" gained by the success of your plans.

Of special importance is the fact that being able to create good plans quickly can provide you with much more time to smell the roses. Good plans tend to clean up your agenda. They provide focus on critical tasks and tend to eliminate tasks that are basically diversions. In this way, more of your agenda can be allocated to the roses.

For me, this means more time for woodworking, hiking, and discovery. Recently, it has also meant rediscovery of a boyhood love—sailing. The promised joy of planning may be the freedom it provides to use your time to smell roses. Similarly, perhaps the grief and pain of best laid plans gone awry involve having to spend your time poorly, having to waste your most precious resource. Fortunately, we can use our metaphorical roses to help us to understand and improve our best laid plans.

Index